CAIRNGOWAN(IV) in ice, St. Lawrence River, Canada.   [Marc Piche Collection]

MEMORIES OF THE CAIRN LINE OF STEAMSHIPS.

AND

NAUTICAL TALES BEYOND LEITH.

GILBERT T. WALLACE.

Doreen,
warmest Regards.
Gil

CONTENTS

DEDICATION.

Dedicated to my wife
Catherine McKinnon WALLACE
and my son
Peter John WALLACE
who have encouraged and
supported my efforts in
the publication of this book
and
in memory of
Joseph BELL
1920 - 2007

FOREWORD.

It has been my great pleasure to sail with 'Gil' on two occasions whilst he was a passenger on the first Q.E.2 and then Q.M.2. during the periods I was in command there. I was most honoured that he asked me to write a brief forward, for this his latest book. Having now had the opportunity to read it and peruse the fantastic photographs and illustrations, I was most struck by Gil's enthusiasm for all things nautical and in particular his vivid and happy memories of his time at sea, with the Cairn Line. The book is written with both humour and meticulous detail. Obviously in producing this work, a great deal of research has been carried out by Gil I have to assume that he must have kept a very comprehensive diary. I have no hesitation in recommending his book to anyone who has any interest in the sea, ships and the crews that sailed them. I have no doubt that it will be of particular appeal to those who have served or are serving in the Merchant Navy. A copy will certainly find a home on my bookshelf. I look forward to sailing with 'Gil' again in the future and at that time, like all retired seamen I am sure that he will be quietly thinking 'it was so much harder in my day' and after reading about his time at sea, it probably was!

Captain Paul Wright.
Master.
Queen Victoria.

QUEEN VICTORIA.

ACKNOWLEDGMENTS.

[Trinity House. Leith]

Credits for the photographs, images, maps and plans are given along with the appropriate entitlement, where the owner of the copyright is known. When not known, attempts were made to trace and obtain permission to re-produce and to give due credit. Inevitably, with older photographs, a few credits are omitted and could not be correctly attributed. For which I offer my apologies. All sketches and paintings, are by the author.

In compiling this book I would like to acknowledge my appreciation for the wealth of information and assistance, freely given by the following:
Audrey Aithchison, Alastair Anderson, John Band, Michael Baxter, Joseph Bell Pearl Brydon, BulletFoto. George Burdon, Ernest Cairns,, John Clarkson, Leith Chamber of Commerce, D.C. Thomson of Dundee, Sharon F. Duffy, Alan Fairley. 'Forth Port PLC,' Marion Foster, 'Fotoflite' Ron French, Neil Gillender, Donald Golightly, Audrey Hindmarsh, Michael Jack, John Landels. Leith Printers. Jack Lenham, John Luke, Mavis Milburn, Edward E. Milburn, Doreen Morris. Peter Redshaw, C.L. Reynolds, Gayle Robinson, 'Scotsman Publications', G.T. Smith, Graeme Somner, Douglas Soppitt, John Stevenson., Charles Sutherland, Dorothy Tweddie, Stanley W. Wilkinson, Peter Wallace., Gordon Wanless, Michael Wright. Finally if I have forgotten anyone and that is not difficult due to the number of individuals that I have contacted or spoken to in preparation of this book, I sincerely apologize and offer belated appreciation.

CAIRNESK(III), Newcastle Quayside.

CHAPTER 1.

INTRODUCTION:

'My previous book 'The Cairn Line of Steamships Co. Ltd. 1876 – 2005.' published in 2005, documents the history of the well known Newcastle-upon-Tyne shipping company, from its earliest beginnings in 1876 and throughout its 129 years history. It includes a chronological history of company, fleet lists, photographs and details of owned, managed and chartered ships and continues to be a popular publication.

This, my second book, also deals with 'The Cairn Line of Steamship' and is created as direct result of the significant amount of interest shown and expressed by many readers into the history of company and of their own connections and affiliations, with it, in the past. The point of focus in this edition however, is predominantly on the 'people', employees and others, including myself, who have previously worked for, or served with, the Cairn Line of Steamships, in the past, rather that with the corporate matters of the company. They all have their own stories to tell. Their personal experiences, employment, recollections and 'tales' are all documented and together provide a representative selection of the careers of the thousands of men who have worked for the Cairn Line over the many years of its existence. Accounts of their careers, some detailed, others not so, some from relatives and others from former crew mates,, Some date from ' the age of sail,' and others from the' twilight years 'of the Company and the 'Mini-bulkers fleet'. All have contributed their details, photographs and a wealth of information, all freely given. Some occurring in times of war, when the courage of merchant seaman, civilians, caught up in dreadful conflict, without any choice, went by unnoticed and others in times of peace, when recession and lay off were, unfortunately, a common occurrence. Collectively documented, I believe they provide an interesting insight into life at sea, with the company, over the last century. Purposely published in an similar format as before, it is hoped that both books will compliment one and other and provide a more complete and comprehensive understanding of history of The Cairn Line of Steamships Ltd.

Also included: Updates for my previous book – The Cairn Line of Steamships Co. Ltd. 1876 – 2005.

A list of Additions and Amendments.
> 'The Last of the Line.' provides a complete history update so far
> on each of the ten' Mini-Bulk carriers and also includes a
> documented index of each vessel mentioned in the text.

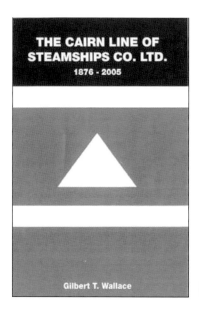

[Also by Author: ISBN.0-9550078-0-1]

CHAPTER 2.

LEITH:' MY HOME PORT'.

I was born at Newhaven, near Edinburgh, in early 1934, and shortly after my family moved the short distance to Leith where I grew up. When I was 15 years old, I attended Leith Academy (Technical) School and then, Leith Nautical College for pre-sea training. So when I joined the Merchant Navy as a Cadet, with The Cairn Line of Steamships, in 1950, I automatically took Leith as 'my home port.' My father was a policeman in Leith and while I was growing up, he would take me for walks into the docks, usually at weekends to see the ships. I soon learned that ships of the' Cairn Line,' were frequent visitors, and I knew their funnel colours, from an early age. Little did I know then, that I would eventually end up going to sea with the Cairn Line and consequently, by the nature of their trade and sailing schedules, would make many return visits to 'my home port', during my time at sea.

Leith has had a long and varied past. At one time just a small hamlet on the shore at the mouth of the 'Water of Leith' The estuary offered a safe haven for ships looking for an anchorage to 'lay up'. In the 1500's a small jetty/pier was erected for the discharge of goods and people. Throughout the years the hamlet of Leith grew in size as did its docks and eventually became the large 'out port' for the City of Edinburgh. During most of the early part of the 20th Century, however, Leith saw a period of rapid decline in its fortunes, industrial decline, mass unemployment and poor housing, all took its toll on the area. It gained an unenviable reputation as a rough, lawless and rundown place. In recent years however, Leith has undergone significant regeneration with massive investment by Forth Ports PLC, City of Edinburgh Council and other Government agencies, which will eventually see Leith port completely closed to shipping and a small town of 17,000 dwellings built in the area of the old docks. I wonder if Thomas Cairns would ever have envisaged such happenings, way back in 1876 at the outset of his venture with the Cairn Line. No matter what changes occur, Leith is and will always remain, 'my home port'

'Atlantic Chambers', former Furness
Withy offices, at Leith.

'Trinity House', Leith.

Leith Tugs: BEAMER, OXCAR and SEALCARR in 2000.

Ships entering Leith – 1824

SIGNAL TOWER. Leith.

The round 'signal tower' (left of middle in previous picture), it is still insitu. In years gone by, the shore ran up to the base of the tower, but in time the then Dock Commissioners reclaimed a vast area of land, to create and develop the present docks system. *[See plan of the harbour and docks].*

LEITH: THE DOCKS.

The 'Western Extension' of the harbour was still tidal until 1969, when the whole of Leith docks were controlled by lock gates and a cofferdam at the extreme North West area of the port complex.

Throughout the years, Leith docks were extended with the building of the Victoria, Albert, Edinburgh and Imperial Docks. Trade also increased with business prospering, as both exports and imports of goods, merchandise, were channelled through the harbour and docks.

A GERMAN TARGET.

[TOM MYLES]

The actual position of the Victoria Shipyard in relation to Leith and Edinburgh as shown in this secret German Luftwaffe map dated October 1939. This clearly shows the intention to obliterate Leith Docks, by aerial bombardment.

POST WAR and THE FUTURE.

The new entrance lock was opened on 28th May, 1969. Prior to this event, the Leith Docks Commission ceased in 1967. On 1st January 1968 the 'Forth Ports Authority' became the official controlling committee, responsible for the administration of ports within the Firth of Forth, namely, Alloa, Bo'ness, Burntisland, Grangemouth, Granton, Kirkcaldy, Leith and Methil and also control shipping to and from the port of Dundee. The Forth Harbour Master and staff are now based at Grangemouth.

Since 2000, 'Forth Port Plc,' have reclaimed more land in the Leith Docks complex. The Ocean Terminal was built on the site of former Henry Robb's, Victoria Shipyard, and at present has approximately 30 cruise ships calling annually. Housing companies have and still are building houses and flats on selected sites throughout the dock complex, also at Granton Harbour. An estimated ten years will see its completion and the overall transformation of the area.

[LEITH CHAMBER OF COMMERCE]

Leith Docks: (looking East). –Showing the 'New Lock' (Bottom left.) and the Western Extension. (Right-foreground).

The regeneration of Leith docklands continues with a proposed 30 storey 100 metres high hotel and flats complex to be known as the 'Edinburgh Tower'. This structure will be the capitals tallest building and be a major part of the Western Harbour redevelopment. Located alongside the Ocean terminal it will provide the focal point of the areas regeneration and future development plans.

Maps, plans & photographs of Leith Harbour & docks, {Past and Present}

1.	Leith harbour.	1681.
2.	Soundings.	1874.
3.	Reclamation dates.	1956.
4.	Entrance to Leith docks: with steamer ST. MAGNUS.	1903.
5.	Entrance to Leith docks.	2006.
6.	Inner harbour.	1905.
7.	Inner harbour.	2006.
8.	The Shore.	1913.
9.	The Shore.	2006.
10.	Upper drawbridge-bascule – S.S BRAESIDE	1900's
11.	Imperial Docks.	1930's
12.	Imperial Docks –Heavy lift crane.- CAIRNESK(III).	1950's
13.	West pier.	1930's
14.	West pier.	2006.
15.	Outer harbour. – West side.	2006.
16.	Western harbour – Extension.	2006.

1. LEITH HARBOUR – 1681.

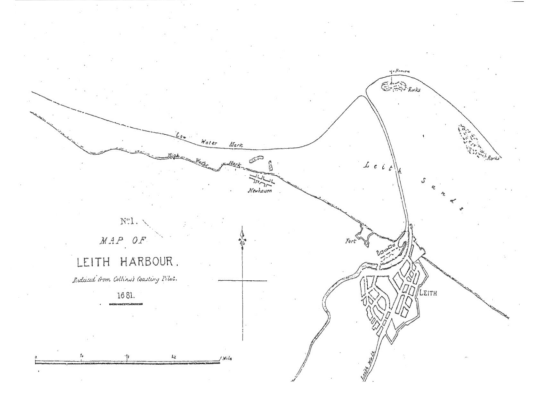

2. LEITH HARBOUR.- 1874.

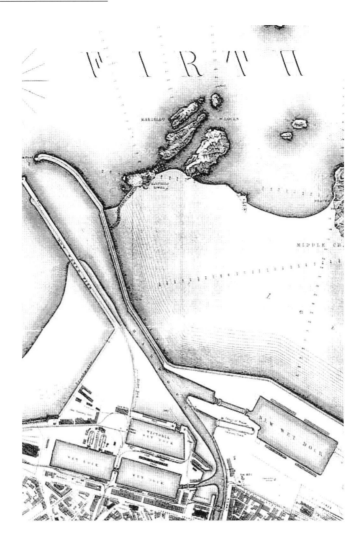

3. Reclamation Dates: 1956.

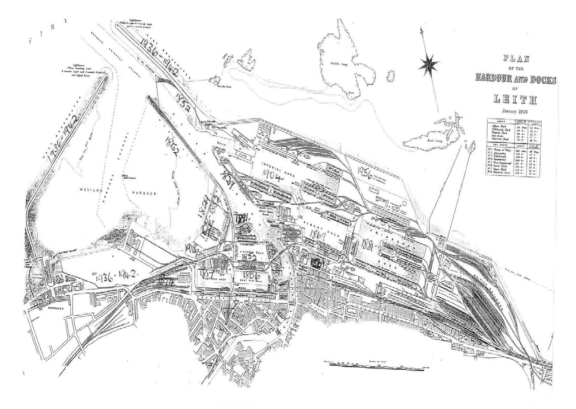

4.

[Entrance to Leith Docks: 1903.]

5.

(Entrance to Leith Docks :2006)

(Inner Harbour: 1905)   [JOHN STEVENSON]

7.

(Inner Harbour: 2006)

8.

(The Shore:1913)

9.

(The Shore: 2006)

Upper Draw Bridge :1900's

These two pictures of the BRAESIDE. Coaster, of Sunderland, A frequent visitor to Leith, show her passing through a bridge, known as the upper drawbridge. It was a lifting bridge known as a Bascule, meaning see-saw (French origin).

BRAESIDE. 390/1909 : Built by John Crown & Co. Sunderland. Y/N.131. for the Wear Steam Shipping Company. (Thomas Rose, Mgrs.) Sunderland.
1929: Renamed VILLE DE TENES for Charles Schiaffino of Algiers.1939,
1939. W.W.II. as Auxiliary Minesweeper AD245.
1945: Returned to 'Schiaffino' and converted to a wine carrier.
11/2/1951. Lost off Sardinia, after fire and grounding.

11.

[Imperial Docks:1930's]   [John Stevenson.]

12.

Imperial Docks – Heavy lift crane-CAIRNESK (III) :1950.'s)

13.

(West Pier:1930'S)   [G. SOMNER]

14.

(West Pier : 2006)

15.

15.

(Outer Harbour : West Side 2006)

16.

(Western Harbour - Western Extension : 2006)

IRON SHIPBUILDING IN LEITH.

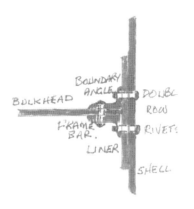

Shipbuilding activities in the Leith area goes back many centuries perhaps even before the GREAT MICHAEL which was built at Newhaven in the 16th Century. Names such as John Sime, Sime & Rankin, James Crawford, Robert Menzies, Lachlan Rose, are but a few of the shipbuilders who operated at various sites in the Water of Leith. Claims of the first dry dock being built in 1720 are extremely doubtful and it is now widely accepted that the first dry dock was built in 1771/1772. Often referred to as John Simes Dry Dock, the outline can still be seen at the open area just south of the Cooperage.

BOUNDRY ANGLE

After the Abbots Bridge was removed, it opened up the upper part of the harbour and Thomas Morton acquired land on the North side of the river below the Junction Bridge on which he developed a shipyard. It was here in 1818 that Morton's Patent Slip was invented and developed. It was much cheaper to build and operate and had many other advantages in that access was better, the light was good and the working conditions were much improved.

Following the completion of the Victoria Dock in 1852, Hugh Morton & Co. later to become S & H Morton & Co. acquired a site to the north of the dock and nearest to the town where they established a more open site. It was here that Iron shipbuilding was begun although others had tried it elsewhere in the harbour. The largest ship built by the company was completed in 1883 as the SCOTIA (2492 grt) for Cyprus Fabre et Cie, Marseilles. Mortons ceased building in 1908 and merged with Hawthorns & Co. Ltd. around 1911.

A business was established in 1846 as Leith Engine Works in Great Junction Street, Leith as Hawthorn & Co. (the main shareholder being William Hawthorn, a Northumberland gentleman, who also had connections with R. & W. Hawthorn Leslie & Co. Ltd., (a major Tyneside shipbuilder). Early work includes the construction of railway engines (sample on display in the Scottish Museum in Chambers Street). Shipyards were established at Granton and later on the South side of the river below Junction Bridge. The shipways on the latter site were angled to make better use of the space both for building and launching. Wooden hulled vessels were built at Granton while the Leith site concentrated on iron although a few wooden vessels were also built at Leith. The company was predominantly builders of fishing vessels but also built a variety of other craft. The business was incorporated as a limited liability company, Hawthorn & Co. Ltd., in 1896 and merged with S. & H. Morton & Co. around 1911. The business was sold in 1924 due to financial problems to Henry Robb Ltd.

John Cran & Co. had an engine works in Tower Street for many years before establishing a shipbuilding yard in 1883 on land adjacent to the Victoria Dock and seaward of S. & H. Morton's yard. This was the middle site of what was to later become known as Victoria Shipyards. In the early days, the company built mainly tugs while continuing to build steam engines for other shipbuilders both in Leith and elsewhere. The business was incorporated in 1917 as John Cran & Somerville Ltd. and continued until 1926 when shipbuilding ceased. The yard was closed in 1927 and the site was acquired a year later by Henry Robb Ltd. The application for a lease of land by Ramage & Ferguson at the outer end of what was later to become Victoria Shipyard, was considered on 10th. March 1877 and signed in April 1877. The shipyard was then established with the first ship launched on 19th. February 1878, named SHAMROCK for the Shamrock Shipping Co. of Larne Ltd. (Manager T Jack), Grangemouth. The yard built many fine ships including the full rigged ship KOBENHAVEN in 1921 for the Danish East Asiatic Co. of Copenhagen, which was lost with all hands in the South Atlantic in 1928. The company was also renowned for its many fine steam yachts. The last vessel to be built (Yard number 269) MERCATOR, an auxillary barquentine, was launched on 9th. December 1931 for the Belgian Government and used as a naval training ship. The company ceased shipbuilding at this time and the site was taken over by Henry Robb Ltd.

Early in 1913, Henry Robb came to Leith and became manager of local shipbuilders, Ramage & Ferguson. In 1918 he left this company to start his own ship repair business. In 1924, Hawthorns went into liquidation and Henry Robb acquired the site that was one of the Victoria Shipyards. He had already built a number of barges and other small craft at a site in Albert Road but soon after occupying Hawthorns Yard, he received a contract to build a dredger for India which was over 200 feet long, too big for the new yard and after discussion with Leith Dock Commission, it was built in the East Commercial Drydock. Robb's purchased the other sites at Victoria Shipyards as they became available and by 1933 controlled the whole of the area. Henry Robb Ltd. and Caledon Shipbuilding & Engineering Co. Ltd., Dundee amalgamated in October 1968 to form Robb Caledon Shipbuilders Ltd and on 1st. July 1977 this company was incorporated into British Shipbuilders. In 1982, the title reverted to Henry Robb Ltd and was finally closed down and dismantled during 1984.

JOHN LANDELS
MASTER MARINER

THE CAIRN LINE : SHIPPING ROUTES.

The N.E. COAST.: 'THIS SIDE OF 'THE POND'

The Cairn Line of Steamships has served the North Atlantic routes with a regular service to and from North East England, Newcastle, Middlesbrough, Leith. Grangemouth and occasionally Dundee to the eastern seaboard of Canada taking in: St. John N.B. & Halifax [winter months only] and including Montreal, Sorel, Three Rivers, Quebec Saguenay River (Port Alfred) & Baie-Comeau all ports on the St. Lawrence River in the Province of Quebec [Summer months only] with services to (Hamilton & Toronto Province of Ontario, after 1956 on the opening of The St. Lawrence Seaway.)[summer months]. Passages varied according to weather conditions but on average took 9 to 11 days with scheduled calls being disrupted with occasional calls to Hull and Sunderland as cargoes dictated.

NEWCASTLE-upon-TYNE. The home port of The Cairn Line of Steamships with the Company's head office situated at Milburn House, Dean Street, Newcastle-upon-Tyne and main loading & discharging point in U.K. for the company's Canadian Service. Outbound journeys to the Canadian Eastern Seaboard, would usually both, commence and terminate at Newcastle Quayside, Berth 26. A regular two vessel service, employed extensively in the transit of freight and general cargo, each ship was, certificated to carry up to 12 fare paying passengers, on the North Atlantic routes

U.K. export cargoes included: iron & steel manufactured goods heavy engineering equipment, chemicals and general cargo with loading ports at Newcastle/ Middlesbrough & Grangemouth). Consumer goods: usually from the C.W.S. and general cargo. (Newcastle) and heavy steel goods and general cargo (Middlesbrough). Bottled whisky was normally loaded at Grangemouth and Leith..

Canadian Imports mainly, bulk commodities, including grain & flour. (Discharging at Leith, and Dunston (Newcastle). Aluminium and copper ingots, (Leith, Newcastle & Middlesbrough). Timber and lumber products (Newcastle) and bulk tallow for Thomas Hedley's soap works in Newcastle and bagged asbestos (Leith and Newcastle) for use in the manufacture of linoleum products.

Voyages commenced at Newcastle and, each ships would take on sufficient bunker coal for the return voyage, to the River Tyne, at either Jarrow Staithes, or the Whitehill Point Staithes at Howden on the North bank of river. Frequently, temporary wooden bunker feeders were constructed, on the top of No. 3 hatch, feeding into the top of the coal bunkers, allowing addition coal to be carried, in order to ensure sufficient supplies for the voyage, particularly in the winter months when severe weather conditions could seriously extend the length of time spent at sea.

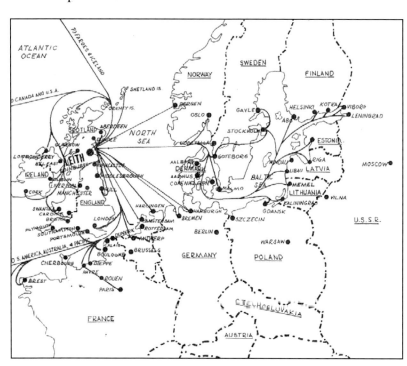

LEITH CHAMBER OF COMMERCE

Routes to and from the Port of Leith, all ports of call in North West Europe, including trade to Faroes, Iceland, Canada, USA, South America, Australia and Pacific.

CHAPTER 3.

THE CAIRN LINE
By George Burdon.

1. We sailed from the Tyne me lads, bound for New-found-land, The decks a-wash the ic-y wind, freez-ing ev-er-y hand; The Plaz-a lights fell far be-hind, I watched them pass and go, Then turned my face in-to the night and the soft-ly fall-ing snow.

CHORUS: For the Cairn Line ships are old, me lads, The Cairn Line ships are few; And in fif-ty three I left the Tyne on board the old Cairn-dhu.

We sailed from the Tyne, me lads, bound
for Newfoundland,
The decks awash, the icy wind, freezing
every hand;
The Plaza lights fell far behind, I
watched them pass and go,
Then turned my face into the night and
the softly falling snow.

CHORUS:

For the Cairn Line ships are old,
me lads,
The Cairn Line ships are few;
And in '53 I left the Tyne on board
the old Cairndhu.

My mother clasped me to her breast, my
sweetheart bade me stay,
But that old Cairn boat was waiting, I
knew I must away;

Away from home and those I loved, to
sail the seas around,
Two years and more would pass away
till I was homeward bound.
From the icy straits of Belle Isle to the
mountains of Peru,
Wherever cargo waited we sailed the
old Cairndhu;
Until one day in Baltimore no cargo
could we find,
So with derricks trimmed and hatches
lashed we turned her for the Tyne.
Standing here in Eldon Square the skies
are cold and grey,
My sweetheart's wed another, I learned
but yesterday;
And the rain has started falling, the
twice-breathed air smells damp,
And I'd sell my soul just to feel the
roll of that dirty Cairn Line tramp.

Best songwriter — twice over

THE OPEN SONG Competition at the
annual Morpeth Northumbrian Gathering
has again been won by George Burdon,
a chief engineer of Chapel House,
Newcastle. The song was judged by
Mrs. P. Clough.

As the best original song entry in the
North-East tradition, it was written
about three years ago after the author
had just visited a friend aboard a cargo
ship in the Tyne. This brought back
memories of the Cairn Noble Shipping
Company which had three or four old
ships running from Newcastle and was
identified by distinctive funnel markings.
The author joined the Cairnavon at
Leith after his apprenticeship and on his
very first night aboard it was ripped
from stem to stern by a fire, three of
the crew died in the disaster.

Despite its wealth of song and
maritime tradition, Tyneside has few
songs about the sea and this is a
welcome addition. In the author's words:
"Like all passing eras, shipping has lost
a lot of interesting characters, both ships
and men, and the Cairn Line had both."

P. Bowron

CHAPTER 4.

THE EARLY DAYS ' On the back of Dolphin'.

Leith Nautical College

In1949, I enrolled at the Nautical College, Commercial Street, Leith. The one year course included a 'term of residence' on board their training ship the T.S. DOLPHIN moored in the Old West Dock at Leith. H.M.S DOLPHIN was built in 1882, by Messrs. Dixon & Company at Middlesbrough as a 3 masted auxiliary barque. Fitted with a horizontal steam engine, she was commissioned into Royal Navy at Sheerness in 1884 and was attached to the Mediterranean Squadron. In 1888 she played a decisive part in the defence of Sukim, Port of Sudan, garrisoned by the British Army. The ship was later involved in suppression of the slave trade in the Mediterranean, until 1896, when she returned to the UK. and was 'paid off' from Naval service and converted into a sea going training ship. Subsequently used as a training ship at Portland and then as the world's first submarine depot ship attached to H.M.S. Mercury at Gosport until 1924 she was decommissioned and sold to be used as a nautical museum at Leith. Towed to the Firth of Forth, in 1925, she was beached at 'Inchkeith,' after 'shipping water ' in heavy seas and for the next 8 months lay awash off 'Fisherrow'. She was then taken into Leith, repaired and berthed in the Old West Dock where instead of her intended use as a museum, was used as a 'boys club' for the youth of Leith. In 1944, after use as a barracks during W.W.2. she was converted into a Merchant Navy training ship providing residential pre-sea training for cadets & deck boys and was leased to Leith Nautical College as T.S. DOLPHIN. She was used in that capacity for the next 30 years, but in 1977, as the needs for such a training facility had diminished and with the impending closure of Leith's Old West Dock, it was decided that she should to be scrapped. On 4th July, 1977, she was towed from Leith Docks, on the short voyage to Bo'ness where she was beached and burnt out, in order to recover the copper cladding from her hull. An ignominious end for such a fine ship which had been 'home', at some time, for many thousands of merchant seamen, including myself!

HMS DOLPHIN. 1882. [Trinity House, Leith.]

[H.M.S. DOLPHIN. Training Ship. Circa.1900's] [Trinity House, Leith]

H.M.S DOLPHIN. 1924: (Beached at Fisherrow)   [TRINITY HOUSE LEITH]

T.S.DOLPHIN 1950's.   [TRINITY HOUSE LEITH]

DOLPIN STRIKERS in 'TRUE MOTION'.

On 4th October, 1950, a 'Decca' Type 159 radar system was installed at the T.S. DOLPHIN for the training of Merchant Navy Officers. The '159' Type radar had just been introduced earlier that year, by the Decca Company of London and was named after the London Transport bus route number which passed the company's laboratory at Brixton, where the radar had initially been researched, developed and then manufactured. It was quite a coup for The Leith Nautical College, to be supplied so early on, with the new type of radar system and at that time it was the only establishment in Scotland providing such a training facility. The 'Decca' Company, (Chinese for 'radar') went on later, to produce the first marine 'True Motion' radar system for which it became world famous.

and ' THE STRIKERS'.

<u>CLASS OF 49.</u>
Back row, left to right: W.CONNOLLY, H.SANGSTER,
I.MCWHANNEL, D.MCILVOGE, B GALLOWAY.
Front *row, left to right:* GIL WALLACE (Author), JOHN YOUNG.

and 'THE SPLICERS'

Left to right: I. R. HIND, Eric EAGLE, Brian GALLOWAY.

and 'THE OARSMEN.'

Boat drill in the Old West Dock.

'THE KNOWLEDGE':   THE INTERNATIONAL CODE OF SIGNALS.

Many years ago I met a cadet who was sitting his 2nd Mate Certificate, at Leith Nautical College. He was looking rather dejected having failed answers to the 'code'. The examiner had told the cadet, to return the next day, to be re examined.

Having written out my 'aid' sometime previously, I gave him a copy and suggested he study it. Within the hour, the cadet was back, whereby I 'examined' him. He passed.

On returning the next day, the cadet was re examined. The examiner told the cadet, that he had not just passed, but passed with 100%. Asked how?, the cadet replied, I met a man who gave me a 'wee haun'. (small hand). The examiner looked at the cadet, but declined to pursue the matter.

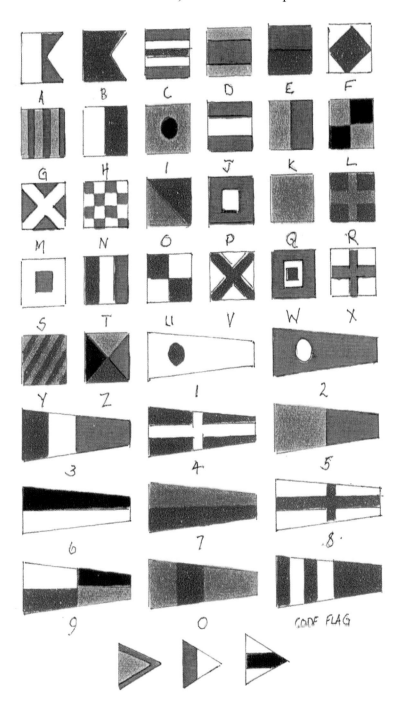

INTERNATIONAL CODE OF SIGNALS.

The set of code flags consists of 40 in number, 26 in alphabetical order o flags, 10 numeral pennants, 3 substitutes and the code pennant signals are made in one-two-three-four letter flag hoists, so placed in alphabetical order, and also the chief words of their corresponding places.

A   I am undergoing a speed trial
        ('Athletic,-first-speed'-trials)

B   I am taking in or discharging explosives
        ('Bang'-dangerous-red-explosives)

C   Yes (affirmative)
        ('C - Si' - foreign language-yes)

D   Keep clear of me - I am manoeuvring with difficulty
        ('D - Difficulty', - keep clear)

E   I am directing my course to starboard
        (I am going to 'writ'e'-right' starboard)

F*   I am disabled - Communicate with me
        ('Fell' - am disabled, speak to me)

G   I require a pilot
        ('Going out of port/harbour', require a pilot)

H   I have a pilot onboard
        (' Entering port/harbour' have a pilot on board)

I   I am directing my course to port
        (' I - 'drink' - port)

J   I am going to send a message by semaphore
        ('J' , man standing with arms outstretched re-semaphore message)

K   You should stop your vessel instantly
        ('K and L' go together - stop)

L*   You should stop. I have something important to communicate

M   I have a doctor on board
        ('M' - Medical or medic, I have a Doctor onboard)

N   No (negative)
        ('N' speaks for itself)

O*   Man overboard
        ('O' - Overboard)

P*   (Blue Peter) in harbour - All persons are to repair onboard as the vessel is about to proceed to sea. (NB - to be hoisted at the foremast head usually 24 hours before actual time of leaving).

Q   My vessel is healthy and I request free pratique
        ('Quarantine' - yellow)

R*   The way is off my ship, you may feel your way past me
        (Go 'Round' me the way is off my ship)

S   My engines are going full steam astern
        ('Speed' engines going astern)

T   Do not pass ahead of me
        (You are the 'vertical' and other ship is 'horizontal' so don't pass ahead)

U*   You are standing into danger
        ('U' are standing into danger)

V*   I require assistance
        ('Arms' outstretched(help)

W*   I require medical assistance
        ('V and W' go together, with 'W' upside down, means 'medical assistance')

X   Stop carrying out your attentions and watch for my signals
        (X means stop, watch for my signals)

Z*   To be used to address or call shore stations
        (The last letter or word, to address or call, (having called ships) therefore it is a shore station).

It should be noted that single-letter hoists refer to important phrases, which are in common use and single letter signals which are only marked with an asterisk should be used by flashing.

'AWAY TO SEA. 'with The Cairn Line:

On the 18th.September 1950, I boarded the CAIRNESK (III) in Imperial Dock, Leith Docks, reporting to Captain John Hogg (relief Master).The 3rd Mate Alan Fairley, took me to the cadets' accommodation on the boat deck-"between the masts". I met the other cadets.

THE OTHER CADETS

Left to right: Bill EVERINGTON, James (Sparrow) WINSHIP , & Don GOLIGHTLY.

I found the accommodation to be reasonable, being well kept, plus hot water (bliss). Cadets in some other shipping companies weren't so lucky. Unfortunately, the' heads were amidships and a long walk in heavy weather.

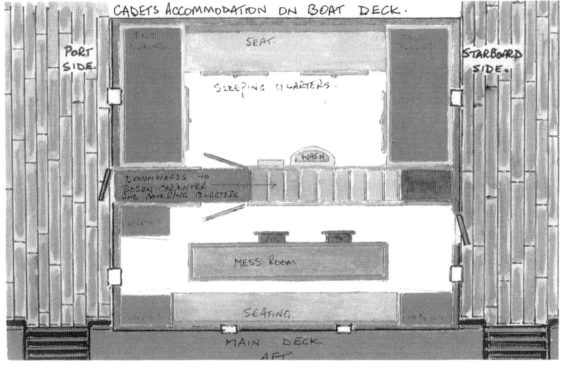

Cadets Accommodation.

FIRST VOYAGE.

I was to learn that the CAIRNESK (III) had been specially designed and equipped for the Cairn-Thomson Line, trade between the UK and Canada to carry general produce. The ship had two decks and a shelter deck. There were five holds with two derricks and two steam winches serving each hold allowing cargo to be loaded and discharged, independent of port facilities. The lower hold was used for bulk cargo and lower 'tween-deck' for general cargo. The 'shelter deck', was fully insulated and brine piped for carrying refrigerated cargo.

'First things first,' I was told how to obtain our food. We were to go outside, forward on boat deck and down steps into the galley, returning the same route. Not the best way in rough weather. This procedure was stopped later, when I tripped and dropped the full dishes, on the steps. After the "accident", we were allowed to use an inside passageway. a much safer and less precarious route.

On 20th September 1950, my 'Big Day, 'arrived! At the Shipping Office in Dock Place, Leith, I signed 'ships articles' and was officially recorded as a 'fully-fledged Cadet.'

We sailed from Leith, 'my home port' that evening, and at 04.00 hrs following morning, I was awoken and instructed to report to the 2nd Mate, at the stern. The weather was 'foul'. It was pouring down with rain, as we entered the mouth of the River Tyne with the pilot onboard. Tugs were fore and aft. As we sailed upstream, I could see the outlines of ships on both sides of the river, with new hulls 'on the stocks', in varying stages of construction. The riverside areas were fully illuminated and the noise of riveting and hammering filled the air. It was deafening, to say the least. I was to learn that the Tyne was one very busy shipbuilding river. We continued on West, up river, past the shipyards and I eventually saw the outline of the Tyne Bridge ahead, and we eventually berthed alongside the Newcastle Quayside some nine miles from the Tyne entrance. Derricks had already been raised and the hatches prepared, ready for the dockers at 08.00hrs all completed under the 'watchful eye' of the 'Bo'sun,' Andrew Guild. That was the first time I met him. I was to find out that he was born at Leith, although he was then living at Perth. He proved to be an excellent seaman, good with the crew and cadets alike and had been a 'loyal servant' of the Cairn Line serving with them for many years. He was to suffer an untimely death, 2 years later, when he fell from the door of a railway carriage into the path of an oncoming train, while travelling home from Newcastle to Perth, for a few days leave, while we were berthed at Newcastle Quayside in 1952.

Andrew GUILD. B.E.M.

HOUNDS BAND

The following day, after breakfast, the other Cadets suggested I should climb the mainmast. On reaching the top up to the truck at the hounds band, I had a great view of the river, to both East and West, especially of the Tyne Bridges, a mile upstream from where we were berthed.

TYNE BRIDGE

The next day, the 25ᵗʰ September,1950, we departed Newcastle Quayside out bound for Quebec/Montreal on my first 'West –bound' crossing of the Atlantic Ocean, to Canada. Four miles downstream, however, we berthed for a short while at Jarrow Staithes on the South bank of the Tyne, to take on coal bunkers. Prior to leaving the Tyne, I was detailed my duties, e.g. clean all brass in wheelhouse, bells, raise wireless ariel, and wire to ships whistle and anything else that needed to be done!

Bunkering took about four hours to complete and then we steamed North from the Tyne and West through the Pentland Firth out into the North Atlantic bound for Canada.

Life at sea would fall into place weather permitting. If rough, lifelines would be rigged in position. During my 4 years, there weren't many trips, where we did not have lifelines in place.

SHIPS WHISTLE

SHIPS BELL

MARLIN SPIKE

WOODEN FID

Other jobs, involved splicing wire ropes and chalking decks with oakum (acumba anglo-saxon) and pitch and of course painting. If it didn't move, paint it!

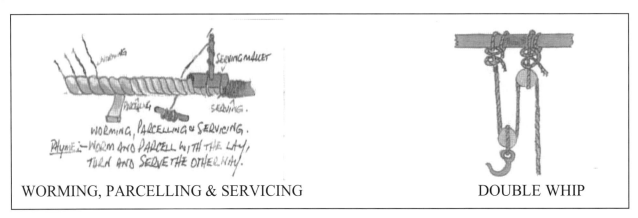

WORMING, PARCELLING & SERVICING   DOUBLE WHIP

<u>FOREIGN PARTS</u>.

As we approached Canada, we would travel one of two ways. First could be by Strait of Belle Isle, the northern point of Newfoundland-Cape Bauld. The second way, south of Newfoundland, Westwards passing Mistaken Point.

FLAG OF CANADA

On approaching Newfoundland we sailed through The 'Straits of Belle Isle' and on into the Gulf of St Lawrence, having first steamed around the North side of Ile d' Anticosti. The town of Port Menier is situated on the West side of the island and has 300 inhabitants. There is a belief that there are 120,000 white tailed deer on the Island.

Then on West round the coast of the Gaspe Peninsular, to the Port of Rimouski to pick up the river pilot. He came out and boarded us from the pilot cutter 'CITADELLE,' before we proceeded Westwards into the St. Lawrence river.

Pilot Cutter : 'CITADELLE.'

We then proceeded on to the City of Quebec, where we dropped off part cargo, which normally took two days to complete. We then continued Westwards, passing The Heights of Abraham and on under the Quebec Bridge before transiting the ports of Three Rivers and Sorel and finally arriving at our final destination, Montreal.

CHATEAU FRONTENAC Hotel at Quebec.

74 GUN SHIP

Note: In 1759, a flotilla of approximately 30 ships under the command of Vice Admiral Charles Saunders landed 9000 troops under command of Brigadier General James Wolfe onto the north shore of the St Lawrence River near to the city of Quebec which had a garrison of 140,00 French troops under the command of General Montcalm.

In September of that year the British army climbed up the cliff face and what was known as the plains of Abraham and attacked the French. Both Wolfe and Montcalm were killed and the French surrendered to the British. The Navy Personnel beside the British Army fought with distinction. In 1763 Canada became British under the Treaty of Paris and in 1775 the Americans tried to oust the British, but were seen off. Later in 1800's the City of Quebec became the capital of Lower Canada-known as Quebec (Province).

BRIDGE AT QUEBEC

From Sorel to Montreal, the St. Lawrence river gets very narrow. In parts you could see vehicles and people moving about. On my first trip, having just passed Sorel, I was standing with Bill Everington on the starboard side of the boat deck. As we watched the shoreline, I mentioned to Bill that I had a premonition of having been here before. Naturally he laughed, but from a headland, still about quarter mile from our starboard midships, which I couldn't see beyond, I described fully the 'location'. I described the buildings, their colours, a church with two spires, school, garage, two warehouses, and a jetty, another large building all down to detail. We just looked at each other in disbelief. Maybe I just had a vivid imagination, and lucky guesses, but I couldn't explain it at all.

As we approached Montreal I noticed a high hill surmounted with a cross, known as Mount Royal. this volcanic plateau is some 550 feet above sea level (Montreal people call it a mountain!). The cross is illuminated during the hours of darkness. As we approached our berth No.4, situated between Quay Alexandra and King Edward Pier, we passed under the Jaques Cartier Bridge.

Jacques Cartier bridge.

The remaining cargo was discharged, over the next few days. prior to us moving across the harbour to load grain, flour and some refrigerated cargo, for the return voyage to the U.K. On leaving Montreal, we entered the Saguenay River for Port Alfred where the cargo was 'topped off' with a consignment of aluminium ingots.

CAIRNESK (III) – at Port Alfred.   [PETER WALLACE]

Battened down for the return journey we dropped off our pilot at Rimouski then East, passing the buoy at Father Point marking the wreck site of the Canadian Pacific's liner EMPRESS OF IRELAND. (14,191g/06) The Glasgow built passenger steamer had sank there on 1st May,1914, with the loss of 1,012 lives after colliding in thick fog, with a Norwegian collier STORSTAD,(6,028g/11) while on an East bound passage from Quebec City for Liverpool. The liners loss ranks second only to the sinking of the TITANIC, two years earlier, in 1912, as the worst disaster in North American maritime history. Time for a quiet moment of refection as we steamed South through the Honguedo Passage through the Cabot Strait and out into the Atlantic bound for Leith. After an uneventful passage across the Atlantic we arrived at Leith, where we discharged part cargo of flour and grain. Then the short trip

CAIRNESK(III) at Imperial Dock, Leith.

around to the Tyne, arriving at Newcastle Quayside, Berth 26. on the 30th November,1950. where I 'signed off' marking the completion of my first 'round trip'. One down, Twenty Seven to go.

AGREEMENT AND LIST OF THE CREW SHIPS ARTICLE
CAIRNESK(III).   Dated: 9/6/1951.- 16/8/1951.

Eng. I.
(80 Men).

AGREEMENT AND LIST OF THE CREW 1951

30 AUG 1951   **FOREIGN-GOING SHIP.**

(Executed in Twenty Pages.)   CRS

The term "Foreign-going Ship" includes every Ship employed in trading or going between some place or places in the United Kingdom and some place or places situate beyond the following limits: the coasts of the United Kingdom, the Channel Islands, and Isle of Man, and the Continent of Europe between the River Elbe and Brest inclusive. For this purpose the term "the United Kingdom" is to be construed as including the Republic of Ireland.

31 AUG 1951
GREENW

Name of Ship	Official No.	Port of Registry	Port No. and Date of Register	Registered Tonnage. Gross.	Net.	Horse Power of Engine N.H.P. I.H.P. B.H.P.
s/s Cairnesk	149412	Newcastle	11 1926	5033	3014	2875

REGISTERED MANAGING OWNER OR MANAGER. Name.	Address. (State No. of House, Street and Town).	No. of Seamen and Apprentices for which accommodation is certified.	CHARTERER. Name.	Address.
Cairn Line Ltd	Milburn House Newcastle on Tyne	51		

The Several Persons whose names are hereto subscribed, and whose descriptions are contained herein, and of whom .... are engaged as Sailors, hereby agree to serve on board the said Ship, in the several capacities expressed against their respective names on a voyage from

of not exceeding ___TWO___ years duration to any ports or places within the line of 75 degrees North and 60 degrees South latitude, commencing at ___LEITH___ proceeding thence to Canada via Tyne and/or any other ports within the above limits, trading in any rotation, and to end at such port in the United Kingdom or Continent of Europe (within Home Trade limits) as may be required by the master.

And it is also agreed, that

(a.) Should any of the crew fail to join at the time specified or fail to be on board at any time or times appointed by the Master he may ship substitutes at once.

(b.) The seamen and firemen shall mutually assist each other in the general duties of the ship.

(c.) The firemen shall keep the galley supplied with coal.

(B3974) Wt. 38668—81, 20M. 1/50. P. & N., Ltd. G813

The crew to work cargo, coal and/or ballast when and where required by the Master

No cash advanced abroad or liberty granted except at the pleasure of the Master.

And the Crew agree to conduct themselves in an orderly, faithful, honest and sober manner, and to be at all times diligent in their respective Duties, and to be obedient to the lawful commands of the said Master, or of any person who shall lawfully succeed him, and of their Superior Officers, in everything relating to the said Ship and the Stores and Cargo thereof whether on board, in boats or on shore; in consideration of which Services to be duly performed, the said Master hereby agrees to pay to the said Crew as Wages the sums against their Names respectively expressed, and to supply them with provisions according to the Scale printed herein.

And it is hereby agreed that any Embezzlement or wilful or negligent Destruction of any part of the Ship's Cargo or Stores shall be made good to the Owner out of the Wages of the Person guilty of the same.

And it is further agreed, that if any Seaman enters himself in a capacity for which he is incompetent he is liable to be disrated.

And it is also agreed, that the additional clauses on pages 2 to 4 and the Regulations authorized by the Ministry of Transport which are printed herein and numbered 1 — 6 incl.

are adopted by the parties hereto, and shall be considered as embodied in this Agreement; and it is also agreed, that if any Member of the Crew considers himself to be aggrieved by any breach of the Agreement or otherwise, he shall represent the same to the Master or Officer in charge of the Ship in a quiet and orderly manner, who shall thereupon take such steps as the case may require; and it is also stipulated that advances on account and allotments of part of wages shall be made as specified against the names of the respective seamen in the columns provided for that purpose.

In Witness whereof the said Parties have subscribed their Names herein, on the days mentioned against their respective signatures.

Signed by .... Master

on the ......9th...... day of ....June........ 1951.

Date of Commencement of Voyage	Port at which Voyage commenced.	Date of Termination of Voyage.	Port at which Voyage terminated.	Date of Delivery of Lists to Superintendent.	I hereby declare to the truth of the Entries in this Agreement and List of the Crew, etc.
9/6/51	Leith	16/8/51.	Newcastle-on-Tyne.	17/8/51.	.... Master.

1. Place S.S. before name if a Steamship, and M.S. if a Motor Ship.
2. Delete inapplicable letters. N.H.P. should always be inserted here if given in the certificate of registry.
3. Here are to be inserted the name and address of any person who has chartered the ship and appoints the Master and Crew, pays their wages, and has for the time being the whole control of the ship.
4. Here are to be inserted the nature and, as far as practicable, the duration of the intended voyage, or engagement or the maximum period and the places or parts of the world, if any, which are excluded.
5. Here are to be inserted the Numbers of any of the Regulations for preserving discipline issued by the Ministry of Transport and printed on the Sixth page hereof, which the parties agree to adopt.
6. Here any other stipulations may be inserted to which the parties agree and which are not contrary to law.
N.B.—This Form must not be unstitched. No leaves may be taken out of it, and none may be added or substituted. Care should be taken at the time of engagement that a sufficiently large form is used. If more men are engaged during the voyage than the number for whose signatures spaces are provided in this Form, an additional Form Eng. 1 should be obtained and used.

Wt. 12937/992 3,500 Bks. 6/50 R.I.Co.Ltd. Gp.773(106)

Short Summary of the Provisions of Section 2 of the Merchant Shipping (International Labour Conventions) Act, 1925, which is required to be included in every agreement with the Crew by Section 2 (3) of that Act.

The employment of a person under the age of 18 in a ship as fireman or trimmer is prohibited except in school ships or training ships specially authorised by the Ministry of Transport or in ships which are mainly propelled otherwise than by means of steam (e.g., auxiliary sailing ships) or under special conditions in ships exclusively engaged in the Indian or Japanese coasting trade.

Where in any port a fireman or trimmer is required and no person over 18 years of age is available, young persons over 16 may be employed, but in such cases two young persons must be employed to do the work which would otherwise be done by one person over 18 years of age.

The Agreement with the crew must contain a list of all members of the crew under 18 years of age with the dates of their birth.

This summary must be included in every agreement with the crew.

List of Young Persons under 18 years of age, and account of all Apprentices employed on board during the voyage.

Name in full.	Date of Birth.	Nationality† (if British, state birthplace).	Capacity.	If Apprentice Particulars of Indentures.		Date of joining for the voyage.	Particulars of Leaving To be filled up by the Master. If remaining it should be stated.		Initials of Official who grants Certificate respecting an Apprentice left behind abroad.
				Date.	Place of Signing.		Date.	Cause of Leaving.	
1. Young Persons* under 18 years of age including Apprentices.									
Gilbert Thomson Wallace	20/2/34								
Geoffrey Holland	9/11/34								
John Hartley	19/9/34								
Wm Everington	30/1/34								
Robert Munro	29·12·34								
2. Apprentices over 18 years of age.									

† If a British subject, state town or country of birth, and if born in a foreign country, state if a natural-born British subject or naturalised.
* In the case of a Young Person (other than an Apprentice) only the name and date of birth need be inserted.

[Twenty Pages

PARTICULARS

Reference No.	Income Tax Code.	SIGNATURES OF CREW AND NUMBERS OF DISCHARGE BOOKS.	Age	*Nationality (if British, state birthplace—see footnote).	ADDRESSES OF MASTER AND CREW — NAME AND RELATIONSHIP OF NEXT OF KIN OR NAME OF FRIEND AND HOME ADDRESS.	Name of last Ship, with Official No. or Port of Registry and year of discharge if more than a year previous.	Date.	Place.
		1095361 (N.I.)			(1) W. Marian		9/6	
1 1912.	M.3	Master to sign first. *Foster* R. 41831	48	London	(2) 44 Newminster Rd. Fenham N'cle	Same	51	Leith
2 1087	M.2	J. Hogg R. 146425.	40	Manchester	(1) W. Eliz G. (2) 26 Waverley St. Wallasey Che.	do	12/6/51	do
3	M.	W. & N. Gordon R. 330167	37	Pembroke Dock	(1) W. Dorothy (2) 41 The Paad Cocta Farm W'l'pool	do	9/6/51	do
4	S	W. P. Wallace. R. 115448	Regd 22	Leith	(1) M. Betsy (2) 17 Pellyside Pae. Edin'. 7	do	do	do
5	—	F. Johnston R. 129275.	38	Ashington	(1) W. Olive (2) 3 Ivy St Amble	do	12/6/51	do
6 3602	M.I	J. B. Jones R. 129275.	42	Edin'	(1) W. Mary (2) 249 St Imechorst Leith	Errington Court	9/6/51	do
7 2451	M.	A Guild R. 410899.	56	Leith	(1) W. Janet (2) Main St. Abernethy	Same	12/6/51	do
8	S	W. Stanley R. 149846.	30	Newcastle	(1) M. Eliz (2) 85 Springfield Rd. N'cle	Same	9/6/51	do
9	M.1	R. C. Pitts R. 216396.	41	Durban S.A.	(1) W. Lily (2) 26 Borough Rd. Sho. Shlds	do	do	do
10	M	A Taylor R. 52856	58	Sho Shlds	(1) W. Jessie (2) 33A Imkehill Tce. Sho Shlds	do	do	do
11	M.2	P. Raymond R. 311033	33	London	(1) W. Mary (2) 164 Bolingbroke St. Scoton Mess	do	do	do
12 1415.	S	J. Armstrong. R. 409859	Regd 18	N'cle	(1) M. Leana (2) 11 Fraig ton, Benwell, N'cle	do	do	do
13 2904	M.2	R. Kitchen 983976	32	HOLLAND	(1) W. Mercy (2) Woodland View Boston Spa Yks	do	12/6/51	do
14 764	M.	J. Cutmore R. 526035	48	Tunbridge	(1) W. Esther (2) — Laugharn St. Newc'l	Per Farm	28/5	Newc'th
15	S	C Glenton R. 549128 (NP)	Regd 18	Grimsby	(1) Sis. Iris (2) 47 Cavendish St. Grimsby	Same	9/6/51	Leith
16	S	P. Eagle (NP) R. 540704	20	Edinburgh	(1) M. Agnes Forbes (2) 2 St Davids St Edin'	do	12/6/51	do
17	S	C. Wallace. R. 524088.	20 2/34	Edin'	(1) F. Peter (2) 17 Pellyside Pae. Edin' 7	Same	9/6/51	do
18	S	D. Golightly R. 528797	Regd 18	N'cle	(1) M. Isabel (2) 101 Glenthorn Rd. N'cle	do	12/6/51	do
19	S	B. Everingdon R. 563325.	30/3	Saltburn	(1) F. Robt (2) 30 Garnet St. Saltburn	do	do	do
20	S	S Holland	9 11/34	Leighton on s	(1) F. Leo (2) The Waterworks Arthington N'r Leeds	Same	9/6/51	do

† The capacities of Engineers not employed on the Propelling Engines and Boilers should be described here and in the Certificate of Discharge as Engine Drivers, Donkeymen.

* If a British subject, state town or country of birth, and if born in a foreign should be described as

‡ If any member of the Crew enters His Majesty's Service, the Name of the King's Ship into which he enters is to be stated under the head of "Cause of Leaving"

‡ If the advance of wages is not conditional on going to sea

** NATIONAL INSURANCE.—The Master and all members of the crew are insurable under the National Insurance Schemes. Masters should ensure that issued by the Ministry of National Insurance.

In what Capacity engaged	No. of Certificate (if any), and No. of R.N.R. Commission or R.V.2. (if any)	Date and Hour at which he is to be on board	Amount of Wages per Calendar Month	Amount of Wages Advanced upon or at the time of Engagement	Amount of Weekly, Halfmonthly or Monthly Allotment	Signature or Initials of Official before whom the Seaman is engaged	PARTICULARS OF DISCHARGE, &c. Date	Place	Cause	Balance of Wages paid on Discharge	RELEASE (Signatures of Crew)	Signature or Initials of Official before whom the balance of Wages was Paid and Release signed and Date	No. of weeks for which National Insurance Contributions are payable	Reference No.
Master	C55 (10) 29720			N.C. Brewery	Engl Sept		16 AUG 1951 NEWCASTLE -ON-TYNE		Remains		C.E. Tate		10	1
1 Mate	C55 58586	from 6/6/51	14 10 -		18 -	J.M.	do	do	Dis.	21 9 1	J. Hogg	A.	10	2
2 Mate	1 M 52637	from 6/6 51	40 - -		26 -	J.N.	do	do	do	12 9 11	W.K.N. Gordon	A.	10	3
3 Mate		from 6/6 51	31 10 -		6 -	J.N.	do	do	do	20 7 5	W.F. Wallace	A.	10	4
R/o	1 Cal 1716.	12/6/51	8 - -			A.	do	do	do	4 1 9	E. Johnston	A.J.	0	5
Carpts		from 6/ 51	31 - -		8 -	J.N.	do	do	do	18 11 1	J.B. Jonson	A.	11	6
Boson		12/6/51	29 -		10 -	A.	do	do	do	19 4 5	A. Guild	A.	9	7
EDH	2486	from 6/ 51	26 -			A.	do	do	di	43 10 11	W. Shanley	A.	C.R.S. 12	8
AB		do	26 -		9 -	A.	do	do	di.	19 13 6	R.C. Pitts	A.	11	9
AB		do	26 -		9 -	A.	do	do	di.	11 12 -	B. Taylor	A.	10	10
EDH	28243	do	26 -		Cancelled	A.	do	do	do	24 2 5	A. Raymond	A.	10	11
EDH	29555	do	24 -		5 -	A.	27.7.51 Newcastle		Dis	17 11 4	A. Armstrong Eng. 2		3	12
AB		12/6/51	26 -		10 -	A.	16 AUG 1951 NEWCASTLE -ON-TYNE		Dis	10 7 3	A. Lataste	A.	10	13
AB		29.6.51	26 -	5 -	8 -	N.	do	do	do	10 12 10	J. Nutman	A.	9	14
J.O.S		from 11/6/51	14 10 -		4 -	A.	do	do	do	5 17 9	C. Glenton	A.	C.R.S. 11	15
J.O.S.		from 12/6/51	14 10 -			N.	do	do	do	10 19 7	E. Eagle	A.	10	16
Cadet		12/6/51	6 16 8			A.	do	do	do	2 11 2	G. Wallace	A.	10	17
Cadet		do	13 - -		2 -	A.	do	do	do	14 8 2	D.J. Slightly	A.	10	18
Cadet		do	13 - -			A.	22.7.51 Newcastle		Dis	2 8 5	Eng. 2		1	19
Cadet		from 10/6/51	6 16 8		4 -	A.	16 AUG 1951 NEWCASTLE -ON-TYNE		Dis	2 6 4	S. Holland	A.	11	20

country, state if a natural born British subject or naturalised.
Refrigerating Engineers, Electrical Engineers, or Winchmen, and not merely as Engineers. Boys entirely employed in connection with the work of Cooks and Stewards
Cabin Boys, not merely as Boys.
the words "not conditional" should be inserted above the entry of the amount.
this Ship," thus "H.M.S. Revenge"; and the other causes of leaving the Ship should be briefly stated thus—"Discharged," "Deserted," "Left Sick," "Died."

National Insurance numbers are shown on seafarers' insurance cards. Details of the National Insurance Schemes as they affect seafarers are given in Leaflet N.I. 24,

PARTICULARS

Reference No.	Income Tax Code	SIGNATURES OF CREW AND NUMBERS OF DISCHARGE BOOKS	Age	*Nationality (If British, state birthplace—see footnote).	ADDRESSES OF MASTER AND CREW — NAME AND RELATIONSHIP OF NEXT OF KIN OR NAME OF FRIEND AND HOME ADDRESS.	Name of last Ship, with Official No. or Port of Registry and year of discharge if more than a year previous	Date	Place
21	M.	*939835* W.B. Hutchinson	56	So. Shlds	(1) W. Karen (2) 1 Rosehill Gdns. Eddis'5	Same	11/6/51	Leith
22	M.1	R.30113 (Eull) A.W. Patterson	29	N'cle	(1) W. Kathleen (2) 3 Denwick Ter. Tynemouth	Same	9/6/51	do
23	S	R.409863	28	Willington Quay	(1) M. May (2) 8 Rothbury Ghs Churchill Estate, Wallsend/Tyne	do	do	do
24	M.	G. Young R.591774	22	Aberdeen	(1) W. Ena (2) 129 Stiffling St., Gateshead	S.R.	25/5	Newcastle
25	S	R.532297 Ref'd D. Rob...	22	N'cle	(1) F. James (2) 76 Wilton Ave. N'cle 6.	Same	9/6/51	Leith
26	M.1	R.405973 Ref'd W.G. Coffman	22	No. Shlds	(1) W. Dorothy (2) 76 William St. Jarrow	do	do	do
27	S.1	R.342908 M.G. Douglas	35	Gateshead	(1) M. Edith (2) 11 Wolsingham Rd Gosforth N'cle	do	do	do
28	M.2	R.27657 J. Creighton	45	Bill Quay	(1) W. Elsie (2) 7 Collingwood St. Hebburn	do	do	do
29	M.2	R.280709 W. Harrison	26	Gateshead	(1) W. Jessie (2) % Ashwood E. Gateshead	do	do	do
30	M.	837235 H. Salmon	56	Rangoon	(1) W. Marta (2) % Park 12 Broughton St. Edinl.	Rubystone	11/6/51	do
31	S.	R.544897 J.J. Barkas	20	Gateshead	(1) Fr. Robt. (2) 49 Vicarian Rd. Gateshead	Same	25/5	Newcastle
32	S.	R.418872 H.M. English	26	Arundale	(1) Mo. Isabella (Marsell) Cumnrland (2) 69 Railway Terr. North Broomhill	do	do	do
33	S.	R.761606 J.P. Dow	74	Newcastle	(1) Fr. John Newcastle Fife (2) 114 Wallsend Rd. Byker	Cardiff	do	do
34	S	R.557415 W. Scott	22	Harton Colliery	(1) Fr. Wily (2) 9 Tenth St. Harton Colliery	W. Voy.	do	do
35	S.	R.548974 D. Dixon	21	South Shlds	(1) Mo. Ann Elizabeth Robson Fulham IV (2) 16 Killing... St. ... Castle Parks	...	do	do
36	S.	R.542172 Wm Douglas	22	Glasgow	(1) Fr. Mary (2) 19 Store St. Glasgow C.	Fulham 16	do	do
37	S.	R.340476 J. Dowle	22	Felling	(1) Mrs. Agnes July 70 (2) 20 Carling... Felling/Tyne	Wave King	29/5	..
38	M1.	R.305634 J. Solig	42	British Honduras	(1) W. Ethel (2) 167 Aberdeen St. Lanark St.	British Fame	..	..
39	S.	R.557416 J. Robinson	24	Jarrow/Tyne	(1) Auntie Mrs. Maggie McCallen (2) 62 Holderness Rd. Jarrow Tyne	1st Voy.	do	do
40	S.	R.557496 (N.I.) M. Thompson	24	Manchester	(1) Mo. Ada Manchester (2) 20 East New St. Old Trafford	1st Voy.	20/6	do

† The capacities of Engineers not employed on the Propelling Engines and Boilers should be described here and in the Certificate of Discharge as Engine Drivers, Donkeymen, should be described as

‡ If the advance of wages is not conditional on going to sea

‡ If any member of the Crew enters His Majesty's Service, the Name of the King's Ship into which he enters is to be stated under the head of "Cause of Leaving"

* If a British subject, state town or country of birth, and if born in a foreign

** NATIONAL INSURANCE.—The Master and all members of the crew are insurable under the National Insurance Schemes. Masters should ensure that issued by the Ministry of National Insurance.

Ship s/s. CAIRNESK

OF ENGAGEMENT

In what Capacity engaged?	No. of Certificate (if any), and No. of R.N.R. Commission or R.N.R. (if any)	Date and Hour at which he is to be on board	Amount of Wages per Calendar Month	Amount of Wages Advanced upon or at the time of Engagement	Amount of Weekly, HalfMonthly or Monthly Allotment	Signature or Initials of Official before whom the Seaman is engaged	PARTICULARS OF DISCHARGE, &c. — Date, Place and Cause of leaving this Ship, or of Death. — Date	Place	Cause	Balance of Wages paid on Discharge	RELEASE (Signatures of Crew)	Signature or Initials of Official	Number of weeks for which National Insurance Contributions are payable	Reference No.
1st Eng.	1 Cl. 59,34	6/6/51	46 10				16 AUG 1951 NEWCASTLE-ON-TYNE		Dis.	113 15 11	W. Dickinson	A.J.	10	21
2nd Eng.	2 Cl. 85601	6/6/51	42 10		15		do	do	do	21 12 -	D.W. Patterson.	A.J.	10	22
3rd Eng.		do	33 -				28 7 51 Aberdeen Dis.			21 7 4	— Eng.2 —		3.	23
4th Eng.		4/6/51	27 10		10		16 AUG 1951 NEWCASTLE-ON-TYNE		Dis.	1 6 11	G. Young	A.J.	9	24
5th Eng.		6/6/51	26 -				do	do	do	6 5 11	D. Robinson	A.J.	12	25
Main Greaser		do	27 -				do	do	do	17 10 4	W.J. Coffman	A.J.	11	C.R.S. 26
Dh Y or		6/51	28 -				29/6/51 GRANGEMOUTH		Mutual Consent	5 6 4	Eng. 2.	A.J.	3	27
Refrig.		6/51	27 10		10		16 AUG 1951 NEWCASTLE-ON-TYNE		Dis.	17 15 5	J. Creighton	A.J.	10	28
Refrig.		do	27 10		8		do	do	do	16 13 7	W. Harrison	A.J.	11	C.R.S. 29
Dh Y or		12/6/51	28 -				do	do	do	32 9 4	H. Sullivan	A.J.	9	30
Fireman and Trimmer		29/6/51	27 10	10	2		do	do	do	8 16 2	J.J. Barker	A.J.	9	31
Fireman and Trimmer		do	24 10	8			do	do	do	14 17 10	H.M. English	A.J.	9	32
Fireman and Trimmer		do	26 10				do	do	do	34 10 11	J.P. Hall.	A.J.	9	33
Fireman and Trimmer		do	21	3 5	2		do	do	do	8 16 -	W. Scott	A.J.	9	34
Fireman and Trimmer		do	21	8	1		do	do	do	5 5 1	D. Dixon	A.J.	9	35
Fireman and Trimmer		22 10		3 5			7/ Montreal		Deserted	- 6 4	ENG 2 A	Jeap	4	36
Fireman and Trimmer		8 am 30/6/51	26 10	7			7/7/51 Plymouth		Hernia Accident	6 7 0	J. Wood ENG.		NIL	37
Fireman and Trimmer		A 26 10		8			16 AUG 1951 NEWCASTLE-ON-TYNE		Dis.	9 15 -	J. Selig	A.J.	9	38
Fireman and Trimmer		8 am 30/6/51	21	3 2			do	do	do	11 10 7	R. Robinson	A.J.	9	39
Fireman and Trimmer		Noon 30/6/51	21	3 2			do	do	do	8 3 3	M. Thompson	A.J.	9	40

country, state if a natural born British subject or naturalised.
Refrigerating Engineers, Electrical Engineers, or Winchmen, and not merely as Engineers. Boys entirely employed in connection with the work of Cooks and Stewards
Cabin Boys, not merely as Boys.
the words "not conditional" should be inserted above the entry of the amount.
this Ship," thus "H.M.S. Revenge"; and the other causes of leaving the Ship should be briefly stated thus—"Discharged," "Deserted," "Left Sick," "Died."

National Insurance numbers are shown on seafarers' insurance cards. Details of the National Insurance Schemes as they affect seafarers are given in Leaflet N.I. 24,

PARTICULARS

Reference No.	Income Tax Code	SIGNATURES OF CREW AND NUMBERS OF DISCHARGE BOOKS 1	Age 2	*Nationality (if British, state birthplace—see footnote). 3	ADDRESSES OF MASTER AND CREW — NAME AND RELATIONSHIP OF NEXT OF KIN OR NAME OF FRIEND AND HOME ADDRESS. 4	Name of last Ship, with Official No. or Port of Registry and year of discharge if more than a year previous. 5	Date and Place of Signing this Agreement. Date. 6	Place. 7
41					(1) (2)			
42					(1) (2)			
43	M.1	1096952 R. N. Dennis	25	Newcastle	(1) 10. Jean (2) 9 Ashleigh Ave. N'cle	Same	11/6/51	Leith
44	S	R. 288902 (N.P.) J. Buzzeo	27	do	(1) M. Jane (2) 14 Gladstone St. N'cle	do	do	do
45	M.	R. 267748 Geo. Elliott	24	Newcastle	(1) W. Jane (2) 56 Walker Road, Byker N'cle	do	do	do
46	S	R. 399916 L. Forrest	19	Gateshead	(1) M. Florence (2) 14 Severn Gdns, Gateshead	do	do	do
	S	R. 577581 Robert Munro	29	St. James Tgh	(1) Ro. Mary (2) 27 Frederick St, Helensburgh	Balaena	28/5/51	Newcastle
48	M.	414340 E. B. Pringle	49	Wallsend	(1) W. Marg'. (2) 8 Waddell R'. Leith	Same	9/6/51	Leith
49	S	R. 419842 J. G. Sinclair	20	Bonar Bdg Sutherland	(1) M. Isobel (2) 13 Tulloch Rd, Bonar Bdge	Skidby	do	do
50	S	R. 528846 John Hadley	19¾	Leith	(1) M. Harriet (2) 76 Albert St. Edin'y	Crichtoun	do	do
51		J. Knaggs	37	Felaw	(1) M. Roseina (2) 38 Tanslwury Gdns, Gateshead	Carmvalona	11/6/51	do
52	S	R. 184526 W. Whitelock	32	Edin'.	(1) M. Jessie (2) 8 Granton Des. Edin'	Rattray Head	do	do
53	M.2	R. 269598 R. W. Chapell	25	do	(1) W. Catherine (2) 268 Canongate, Edin'	Dunkery Beacon	do	do
54	M.1	R. 549143(N.P.) W. O'Hara	29	Blantyre	(1) W. Catherine (2) 40 Whitson Walk, Edin 11	First	12/do	do
55	S	R. 544887 J. J. Barkas	20	Gateshead	(1) F. Robt (2) 49 Acacia Rd, Gateshead 8	Poole Harbour	do	do
53	S	R. 544908 C. Begg	23	do	(1) M. Kathleen (2) 28 Holly Ave, Gateshead 11	Same	do	do
57	M.2	R. 269028 John Thompson	26	Dunston	(1) W. Mary (2) 9 Dorothy St, Gateshead 8	do	do	do
58	S	R. 533340(N.P.) J. Snell	22	Ludworth Co. Durham	(1) M. Emma (2) 14 Barnet Ave, Ludworth, Durham	First	do	do
59	S	R. 544841 R. Johnston	23	Musselburgh	(1) M. Mathilda (2) 10 Whitecraig Rd, Musselburgh	Cadanwood	do	do
60	S	R. 549078 William Rose	27	Bathgate	(1) F. John (2) 6 Crofefield Pl. Broxburn	Same	do	do

† The capacities of Engineers not employed on the Propelling Engines and Boilers should be described here and in the Certificate of Discharge as Engine Drivers, Donkeymen.
* If a British subject, state town or country of birth, and if born in a foreign should be described as
‡ If any member of the Crew enters His Majesty's Service, the Name of the King's Ship into which he enters is to be stated under the head of "Cause of Leaving" ‡ If the advance of wages is not conditional on going to sea
** NATIONAL INSURANCE.—The Master and all members of the crew are insurable under the National Insurance Schemes. Masters should ensure that issued by the Ministry of National Insurance.

M. M. OFFICE
17 AUG 1951
NEWCASTLE-ON-TYNE

In what Capacity engaged	No. of Certificate (if any), and No. of R.N.R. Commission or R.V.R. (if any)	Date and Hour at which he is to be on board	Amount of Wages per Calendar Month	Amount of Wages Advanced upon or at the time of Engagement	Amount of Weekly, Half-Monthly or Monthly Allotment	Signature or Initials of Official before whom the Seaman is engaged	Date	Place	Cause	Balance of Wages paid on Discharge	RELEASE — Signatures of Crew	Signature or Initials of Official before whom the balance of Wages was Paid and Release signed and Date	Number of weeks for which National Insurance Contributions are payable	Reference No.
Fireman and Trimmer														41
Fireman and Trimmer							16 AUG 1951							42
		noon 6/6/31	35 - -			H.	NEWCASTLE-ON-TYNE	do	dis.	25 13 9	R N Dennis		10	43
		11/6/5.	23 10 -				do	do	do	23 7 3			10	44
		noon 6/6/31	25 - -				do	do	do	10 12 10			11	45
		6/6/31	22 - -				do	do	do	4 12 10	R S Francis		11	46
		31					do	do	do	6 13 2	R Munro		10	47
	11367	6/6/31	32 - -				do	do	do	10 12 3	O B Pringle		10	48
			21 10 -				do	do	do	1 -	J Sinclair		10	49
		noon 7/6/51	11 - -				12/6/51	Leith	dis	1 18 3	M 3 Leith		2	50
		noon 11/6/31					7 JUL 1951 GRIMSMOUTH	dis	nil				0	51
		noon 12/6/51	26 10				13 JUN 1951 NEWCASTLE-ON-TYNE	dis	3 16 7				0	52
Y. S.		do	26 10 -				do	do	do	3 16 7			0	53
Y. S.		do	21 - -				do	do	do	3 4 4			1	54
Y. S.		do	22 10 -	plus N.M.B.			do	do	do	3 6 4			1	55
Y. S.		do	22 10 -	Run Bottes LEITH To			do	do	do	3 6 4			1	56
Y. S.		do	26 10 -	NYCLE only.			do	do	do	3 11 8			1	57
Y. S.		do	21 - -				do	do	do	3 4 4			1	58
Y. S.		do	22 10 -				do	do	do	3 6 4			1	59
Y. S.		do	21 - -				do	do	do	3 4 4			1	60

country, state if a natural born British subject or naturalised.
Refrigerating Engineers, Electrical Engineers, or Winchmen, and not merely as Engineers. Boys entirely employed in connection with the work of Cooks and Stewards
Cabin Boys, not merely as Boys.
the words "not conditional" should be inserted above the entry of the amount.
this Ship," thus "H.M.S. Revenge"; and the other causes of leaving the Ship should be briefly stated thus—"Discharged," "Deserted," "Left Sick," "Died."

National Insurance numbers are shown on seafarers' insurance cards. Details of the National Insurance Schemes as they affect seafarers are given in Leaflet N.I. 24,

[Twenty Pages

PARTICULARS

Reference No.	Income Tax Code	SIGNATURES OF CREW AND NUMBERS OF DISCHARGE BOOKS.	Age	*Nationality (if British, state birthplace—see footnote).	ADDRESSES OF MASTER AND CREW — NAME AND RELATIONSHIP OF NEXT OF KIN OR NAME OF FRIEND AND HOME ADDRESS.	Name of last Ship, with Official No. or Port of Registry and year of discharge if more than a year previous.	Date	Place
		1	2		3	4	6	7
61	S	R.226889 7 Scott	30	Edinburg	(1) Mrs. Helen (2) 45 Wallyfield ... Edinburgh (1) Son Stanley William Edinburgh	Benjamin	6 7·8·51	Newcastle
62		Karen E. Wilkinson	51	Leith	(2) 1 ... Edin Trinity (1) ...	St Ivy	do	do
63	S	R.504790 Matthew R Lockhart	18	Wellington	(2) 28 ... Colin, Wardley	Ashdown	do	do
64	m	R Johnson	53	N Shields	(1) W. Kenn (2) 18 Chiswick St N. Shields	Same	30/6/51	do
65	m7	G Dunn R230036	47	N Shields	(1) W. Margaret (2) 16 Blackthorn ... N.S.	Cinnamon	do	...
66	m1	Harold Cochrane R551653	28	Uddingston	(1) Wife Elizabeth 10 South Street Uddingston (2) 2 South St Uddingston	Repton	3/7/51	Grangemouth
67	52	D Fidet R280000 (NP)	28	Cambuslang	(1) Mother Jeanie (2) 44 Dukes Rd Cambuslang Lanarks	Saint Rosary	do	do
68	S	D. McLelland R509820	37	Lochgelly	(1) Sister Janet Lisette 123 Plantation Street, Lochgelly (2) Same address	British Security	do	do
69	52	W M Clatton R539784	29	Grangemouth	(1) Mother Marjory (2) 57 Lime Street Grangemouth	Great Field	5/7/51	do
70	S	T F Flynn	39	Lauriston	(1) Mother Joan (2) 46 Almond Street Lmouth	Dynamo	7/7/51	do
71	S.1	A H King R172250	35	Port Comwall	(1) Mrs McLaing (2) 23 ... House Lmouth	Security	7/7/51	Montreal
72	S	Lennigan R.518819	30	Burnt Island	(1) Mother Mrs Elizabeth Dunnigan (2) Ballie St Leith	Ryloe	15/8/51	Leith
73					(1) (2)			
74					(1) (2)			
75					(1) (2)			
76					(1) (2)			
77					(1) (2)			
78					(1) (2)			
79					(1) (2)			
80					(1) (2)			

* If a British subject, state town or country of birth. and if born in a foreign

† The capacities of Engineers not employed on the Propelling Engines and Boilers should be described here and in the Certificate of Discharge as Engine Drivers, Donkeymen, should be described as

‡ If any member of the Crew enters His Majesty's Service, the Name of the King's Ship into which he enters is to be stated under the head of "Cause of Leaving

‡ If the advance of wages is not conditional on going to sea

** NATIONAL INSURANCE.—The Master and all members of the crew are insurable under the National Insurance Schemes. Masters should ensure that issued by the Ministry of National Insurance.

Ship S/s Cairnesk

OF ENGAGEMENT							PARTICULARS OF DISCHARGE, &c. To be filled in by the Master upon the Discharge, Death, or Desertion of any Member of his Crew.				RELEASE		Number of weeks for which National Insurance Contributions are payable	
In what Capacity engaged.	No. of Certificate (if any), and No. of R.N.R. Commission or R.V.R. (if any)	Date and Hour at which he is to be on board.	Amount of Wages per Week or Calendar Month.	Amount of Wages Advanced upon or at the time of Engagement	Amount of Weekly, Half-Monthly or Monthly Allotment.	Signature or Initials of Official before whom the Seaman is engaged	Date	Place	Cause	Balance of Wages paid on Discharge.	We the undersigned Members of the Crew... Signatures of Crew	Signature or Initials of Official before whom Wages was Paid and Release signed and Date		Release No.
8	9	10	11	12	13	14	15	16	17	18	19	20	21	
3.d.Eng		4.6.51					16 AUG 1951 NEWCASTLE-ON-TYNE 15/8/51		Dis	22 5 1	t Scate	H	11	61
Engr		28.6.51	1				51	Leith	Dis	—	Eng 2		0	62
C'Room		19.6.51		0	Half		16 AUG 1951 NEWCASTLE-ON-TYNE		Dis	Nil	M. Lockhart.	At	10	63
Supt	F.J	3?/6/51	1				17/51	Smouth	dis	n.c	Eng 2 Smouth Jeff		NIL	64
do	do		1				1/7/51	do	dis	n.c	— do —	Jeff	NIL	65
Fireman		3/7/51	26 10	5 5 — 1 5 0			16 AUG 1951 NEWCASTLE-ON-TYNE		Dis.	17 17 —	Thomas Lockwood	M.	8	66
E.D.H	30632	do	26	3	1/2 M 4		do	do	do	18 2 5	L. Finlet.	H	8	67
Fireman J.		do	26 10	5	1/2 M 4		do	do	do	14 2 5	D. McLelland	H.	8	68
Fireman J.		4/7/51	24 10	3	1/2 M 6		do	do	do	13 6 5	W m Blaff t	H.	8	69
F&T		1:7.51	26 10	8			13 AUG 1951 LEITH		Dis	15 16 6	Eng 2		7	70
F&T.		4/3/51					16 AUG 1951 NEWCASTLE-ON-TYNE		dis	9 17 10	A R Sirb	H.	3	71
F&T.		15/8/51	26 10 —				do	do	do	2 11 8	J Rumigen	L.	1	72
													73
													74
													75
													76
													77
													78
													79
													80

CHAPTER 5.

RECOLLECTIONS.

On the numerous crossings that followed my 'first trip', some every day events occurred, which to me, as 'fledgling' cadet, were all new and worthy of note:

PORT HAND BUOY
(CHANNEL)

When Cadets were on duty at holds watching the loading or discharge of specific cargo, they would be paid overtime over their normal hours.

During our stay in Newcastle, the ships chippy carpenter reported to the first mate that there appeared to be rust in a couple of the cellular double bottoms. So guess who ended up going down into the hold? Bill and I with the chippy (carpenter). We opened up the two tanks, sure enough there was brown water, so Bill and I got started. We climbed into and swabbed the tanks until dry, chipping away the rust. We then red leaded the double bottom compartment where upon the chippy ok'd our work and screwed down the covers. Bill and I were glad there were only two tanks to do.

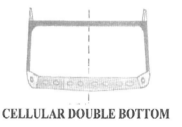

CELLULAR DOUBLE BOTTOM

I found out that Newcastle Upon Tyne was first known as Gorebridge by the Romans. It was at the east end of Hadrians' Wall, A bridge at the east end of the Tyne – the Pons Aelius Fort on the north side of the bridge-settlement that became Newcastle. It was to believed to be called Manchester-Fifth Century.

WHISKY GALORE!

One time in Montreal, we had a large consignment of whisky in No 2 and 4 holds, we Cadets would again take turns watching the unloading and change every hour. One time, I had just taken over at No.2 hold, and the stevedores had returned after their lunch break. After a while, I noticed a man standing at the hatch coaming, looking into the hold. A stevedore told me later, that the man was the company boss. The boss shouted down into the hold to one of the stevedores, whereupon the docker came up onto the deck. I saw that possibly the docker had had a refreshment during his lunch break. I hadn't seen anything untoward re breakages etc. but after some words, the stevedore left the ship. Within 10 minutes, another man appeared taking the dismissed man's job (jobs were hard to come by). I was later told that the first stevedore had been paid off for being under the influence of alcohol, but there was no mention that he had tampered with the cargo.

BUCKET OF SCOTCH.

One trip, we loaded thousands of cases of whisky at Leith and Grangemouth for transport to Montreal. The Cadets had to watch each hold, when whisky was being loaded. On occasions, whether accidental or deliberate, you could never be sure, but someone always produced a bucket, or can, to catch the whisky that poured from a dropped case. In Grangemouth, one time, about 0300hrs some crew members tried to enter a secure part of No 4 hold, naturally to get at the whisky. The plot was blown. I think the seamen were drunk or stupid or maybe both, anyway, all the Deck Officers attended and went down into the hold. My brother Bill was 3rd Mate at the time and as he entered the hold, he stepped on some dunnage (wooden spars). Well, Bill was a big lad and quite heavy, by which there was a shout from underneath the donnage. One of the seamen had hidden himself but unfortunately, Bill had stepped on him, however, the seamen never got any whisky.

HATCHWAY

FRENCH HOSPITALITY.

One trip to Montreal we berthed at the oil berth for a couple of days. Arthur and I went ashore and during the evening we met some of the crew, and later we went into a club, where initially, we were made welcome. The 'chippy' (carpenter) and 2nd Cook, on coming back from the 'heads,' the cook was laughing at one of chippy's corny jokes. But alas, the club was playing 'La 'Marseillaise' (wrong time for laughter). The French members thought we were taking the 'mickey' – result, a fight. Somehow the members managed to encircle us and push us all out through the door. We walked away from the club for about four blocks. As we all sat on a grass verge, two police cars arrived and questioned us about an alleged disturbance at the club. Being sober, I was put forward as spokesman so I explained what happened. The senior Police Officer accepted our explanation and said not to go back to the club, as it had a bad reputation. I thanked them on behalf of the boys, where upon the officer said he would give us a lift back to our ship at the oil berth, for which we were very thankful, as it was quite a distance. We thanked the officer profusely for everything, whereupon he said to forget it and to have a good trip home, as we were leaving the next day.

Anyway, in the morning we heard police and ambulance arriving at the stern of the CAIRNESK (III). A body had been found in the river at the stern of our ship, and as the ambulance and police tried to extricate the body from the water an arm came off. Eventually the officers managed to retrieve the body. As it was being brought up, naturally there was a crowd of crew, watching from the stern. As the body came into view the 2nd Cook said "he's got a good pair of shoes on him". So much for seamen's humour.

After loading up with grain and bagged flour, we would move down the St Lawrence River, occasionally diverting northwards into the Saguenay River for Port Alfred to load aluminium ingots from the smelter. At the junction of these two rivers it was great to see the numerous types of mammals frequenting these waters. I saw dolphins, minkie, finback and beluga whales, and killer porpoise. There seemed to have been an abundance of them in the St. Lawrence river at that time. The Saguenay river is approximately 65 miles long and about a quarter of a mile wide in places, varying from 300 feet to 1000 feet in depth and the precipitous cliffs were about 500 feet to 1700 feet in height. Approximately twenty miles upriver on the West side there is a statue of the Virgin Mary. It was situated half way up a rock face, I don't know if it was originally transported by boat or lowered from the top of the cliff. It was very imposing.

STARBOARD HAND BUOY

KNOCK OUT.

In 1951, on our way home, during my third trip, we passed the Butt of Lewis in very heavy weather, sailing East through the Pentland Firth, when a very unfortunate accident occurred. The Bosun, Andrew Guild had sent Cadet James (Sparrow) Winship to the stern locker to get some material. The ship was pitching and rolling very heavily, so when Winship got to the stern he opened up the metal locker door and hooked it back against the bulkhead. He entered the locker room and went down the wooden steps. On coming back up, we believe he stepped down onto the step, but the stern went further down due to the swell. As the stern rose up, he missed his footing, throwing him backwards. He landed on the metal deck, being knocked unconscious. After about five minutes, the Bosun wondered what was keeping Winship so he went aft and found him lying in the locker room. Immediately the Bosun and two Seamen carried him along to the Chief Steward, informed the Captain and Winship was placed in an empty passengers cabin. The Radio Officer wired ahead and we headed for the Port of Leith. On our arrival Winship was transferred to Leith Hospital for examination and treatment. Later the same day the Captain asked me to go to Leith Hospital to ascertain the condition of Winship. At the hospital, I found that he was okay, but would be kept in for a few days observation.

Cuthbert left the CAIRNESK (III) after another trip and joined the Blue Star Line as a cadet. The vacancy was taken by Cadet Geoffrey Holland.

Geoff, Gil and Don.   Bill Wallace & his brother Gil.

Montreal- 1952.

BAY OF FUNDY.

Our voyages in winter, were interesting. On my first trip to St. John New Brunswick, I learned that the Bay of Fundy was known for having the highest tidal level in the world.

We experienced this on several occasions while berthed in St, John with a bore moving up the River Petticodiac. We never saw a high bore, mostly 1 to 2 feet high. As a bore runs up the river, and the river shores get nearer, the water surges onto the embankments with enormous energy of power. As it reaches the inland neck of the river, the bore has increased in size and can devastate the shoreline on both sides. Many years ago, 300 acres were devastated, with approximate loss of 200 people, caused by an enormous bore.

The size and height of the bore is determined by the tide, itself regulated by the moon.

NIGHT SNOW MEN.

During the winter of 1952, we arrived in St John N.B. on CAIRNESK, when Bill and I opted to act as night watchman, (overtime of course), between 17.00hrs and 08.00hrs. We had been berthed in the harbour for a couple of days, when the weather 'took a turn for the worse.' It was very cold and during our third night watch, it started to snow heavily. After two hours or so, of falling snow, the ship was completely covered to a depth of 3 feet. We decided to inform the 1st Mate who in turn, told us to call out the Bosun, and all deckhands who had to forsake their 'donkeys breakfasts' for a cold snow bound deck. By 04.00hrs everyone was on deck and shovelling the snow over the side, into the harbour. By this time the ship had actually developed a slight list to starboard, but after two to three hours of shovelling and scraping, the ship was cleared of snow and the list corrected.

["The morning after the night before"]

TUNNEL OF FOG.

During the same trip, we encountered heavy fog, approaching the south tip of Newfoundland-Mistaken Point. There was a seaman on lookout in the bows, and I was on the monkey island. The 3rd Mate informed us, we were about ten miles off Mistaken Point, on our starboard bow, and the fog became thicker. The bowman and I saw at the same time, what appeared to be a 'tunnel' through the fog. The fog had closed down around us, but this 'spectacle of tunnel' was clearly seen, sometimes called a 'bore hole.' I blew down the mouth pipe to the 3rd Mate. He and the helmsman had also saw this 'apparition'. At the end of the 'tunnel' was Mistaken Point-about eight miles distant. The 3rd Mate obtained a reading, and then the 'tunnel' closed up, fog all around us. Incidents like this happen which no one can explain but all you can do is marvel at seeing them.

The following photographs of voyages over the North Atlantic varied greatly regarding the weather-from reasonable to heavy severe and at times coupled with ice and snow.

CAIRNESK (III) 1940's

CAIRNESK(III) 1950's

CAIRNESK (III) 1950's   [three above images- ALAN FAIRLEY]

GRAND BANKS: TITANIC.

On our voyages crossing the North Atlantic, we experienced ice and fog. The area of the Grand Banks, South of Newfoundland and East of Nova Scotia was especially hazardous to shipping. When sailing, westwards over this route, I would think of the inhuman tragedy of the sinking of the R.M.S TITANIC (Sunday 14th April, 1912 – position 41° 46'N 50° 14'W – call sign MGY). Many of the survivors were conveyed to Halifax N.S. Later in the 1980's I read a book giving a very good account of the tragedy in an excellent biography; called *"Titanic Voyager, The Odyssey of Charles Herbert Lightoller"* by Patrick Stenson. Lightoller was the second officer onboard the TITANIC, and Senior Deck Officer at the Enquiry.

METAL TO METAL.

In 12th January 1953, CAIRNESK (III) was entering St. John harbour, New Brunswick. Two tugs had lines attached, one at the bow and the other at the stern. A cargo ship, NOVAPORT was berthed, on our starboard. A second ship, the 'Liberty ship' KYLE V. JOHNSON was berthed on the opposite quay, to our portside. It was our intention was to berth ahead of the NOVAPORT, starboard side to the wharf. The Captain, 3rd Mate and pilot were on the bridge, with myself on the helm. As we entered the dock, our bows started moving to our starboard. I applied the helm to port, no response.

We started to move towards the NOVAPORT the Captain and Pilot on seeing this happening instructed me to put the helm to starboard and rung down by the telegraph to the engine room to go in reverse. In theory, this action would take us astern away from the NOVAPORT. Also both tugs were endeavouring to keep us away from the NOVAPORT. As this happening, the 3rd Mate on our bridge saw backwash coming from the berthed ship on our port side. (They were in fact testing their propellers by reversing them). No one was in attendance on the after deck (stern) of this ship.

The CAIRNESK (III) continued to move to starboard, regardless of our endeavours to prevent this. The tugs tried to keep us from moving to starboard, away from the NOVAPORT. They did manage to slow us, but the back wash was very strong, whereupon our starboard bow struck the port bow of the NOVAPORT. We moved backwards, causing our starboard bow to scrape along the port side of the NOVAPORT. I heard a couple of load cracks, which were in fact her two wire springs snapping.

As we continued to scrape down the port side of the NOVAPORT, their officers and crew were dashing up onto their decks, wondering what was happening. After it was all over, we moved forward into our berth ahead of the NOVAPORT. The arguments went on during the night between our ships officers, personnel and the other ships involved. Believe it or not, but it was over a year before I was called to a solicitors office in Newcastle to give a statement.

LLOYDS WEEKLY CASUALTY REPORT S20/1/1953, noted damage as follows:
CAIRNESK (III) Starboard Hawse pipe broken and shell plate inway was torn.
NOVAPORT one shell plate slightly dented, minor damage to port bridge wing.

Note: The NOVAPORT is not shown in the above photograph, which was taken, two days after the 'collision', by which time the NOVOPORT had sailed from the port. The vacated berth, behind the CAIRNESK, was then occupied by the white hulled, Canadian flagged, cargo ship. CANADIAN CHALLENGER.(6,745/46.) as shown.

THE HALIFAX EXPLOSION

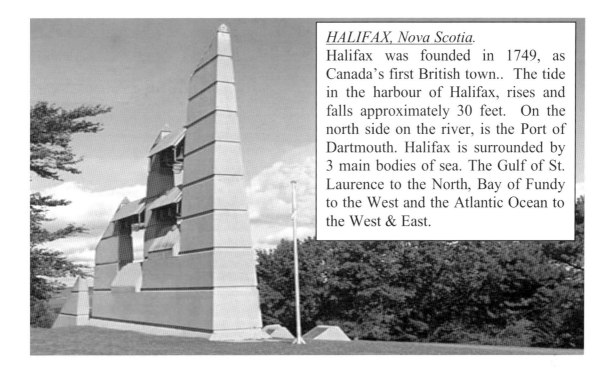

HALIFAX, Nova Scotia.
Halifax was founded in 1749, as Canada's first British town.. The tide in the harbour of Halifax, rises and falls approximately 30 feet. On the north side on the river, is the Port of Dartmouth. Halifax is surrounded by 3 main bodies of sea. The Gulf of St. Laurence to the North, Bay of Fundy to the West and the Atlantic Ocean to the West & East.

THE TWO SHIPS!

Norwegian Steamer. IMO, grounded after the explosion at Halifax in 1917.

French Steamship. MONT – BLANC.   Halifax 1917.

On 29th December, 1950, CAIRNESK put into Halifax, Nova Scotia, on the first call of the 'winter schedule'. This was my first visit to the city with its huge natural harbour and 'bottleneck' entrance known as 'The Narrows'. While talking with dockers unloading the ship, they told me about the 'Great Explosion' of 1917 and the devastating effect it had on the people of Halifax. This prompted me to find out more about the incident, while I was there. In the Fairview Cemetery, overlooking the harbour, there was a monument to commemorate 'The Unidentified' of the 'Great Disaster' as well as the graves of hundreds of other people killed during the explosion. I was also to learn that 125 victims of the sinking of the Titanic five years earlier in 1912 are buried in the same cemetery. A poignant reminder to myself, as we had steamed near to the position of the sinking of the Titanic a few days earlier, during our trip across the North Atlantic to Halifax. Unfortunately my stay in Halifax was short, but in that time I had learned how the people of Halifax had, seen more than their fair share of tragedy, during the city's short history.

The Halifax explosion of 1917 devastated the port and City of Halifax,, Nova Scotia resulting in the deaths of over 1,600 people and the wounding and injuring of 9,000 others. Halifax was at the time booming and was at the centre of the Canadian immigrant trade with displaced persons entering into Canada from Europe. The onset of WW1 had also turned the port into an important naval base and cargo handling facility. Its huge natural protected harbour and important railway connections into Canada and the United States of America had prompted unparalleled expansion in trade, industrial and residential growth. Optimism was high with prospects for further expansion as the impetus of WW1 escalated and the demands on the city and harbour facilities increased. With the movement of troops and military hardware for the 'The Western Front', the port became not only an increasingly important distribution centre and departure point for troops but also a crucial convoy assembly point for ships leaving for Europe. Ironically, the war in Europe was proving an economic blessing for the city and its ever increasing population, (over 50,000 souls at the time of the disaster) and the prospects for future expansion and wealth looked good. To this back drop came the most devastating event in the City's history. At 8.45am on the 6th of December, 1917, a collision occurred at the harbour mouth, known as 'The Narrows' between an unloaded Norwegian cargo ship IMO.(5,043g/1889) which was leaving the harbour, and a French cargo vessel MONT-BLANC (3,122g/1899) loaded with a cargo of almost 3.000 tons of 'munitions' and explosives (Picric acid, T.N.T. and drums of benzole) which was attempting to enter the harbour's inner basin. The impact of the collision caused a fire amongst barrels of benzole stored on the fore deck of French cargo ship. Unable to reach the fire fighting equipment and aware of the dangerous cargo on board, the crew abandoned ship on the Captain's orders leaving the blazing vessel drifting helplessly towards the Halifax shore. At this stage crews from Royal Navy and Canadian Navy vessels in the harbour began tackling the blaze unaware of the steamers lethal cargo. Attempts were made to tow the blazing ship out of harbour when just twenty minutes after the initial collision, the cargo of the MONTE-BLANC exploded in one of the world's largest ever man made explosions. The city was decimated. Churches, schools, dwelling houses, factories, docks and ships were totally destroyed by the effect of the blast. Large groups of workmen, children on their way to school and people watching the disaster enfold, unaware of the impending danger, were killed outright by the effects of the blast. Thousands of others were to suffer horrendous eye injuries, blinded from flying glass, wooden splinters and shrapnel. Over 325 acres of North Halifax were totally destroyed by the blast, fires and the ensuing tidal waves. It took over 2 months before the remains of the deceased could be buried, many of their identities unknown. Within a year, shortly after the 'Armistice in Europe', had brought an end to the First *World War,* the 'Halifax Explosion' death toll had risen to in excess of 2000 souls, with over 9.000 injured. Relief came from all around the world with over 28 million dollars being eventually collected as aid for the victims and to rebuild the devastation caused to the city. Gradually Halifax was rebuilt. The long ensuing legal battle to apportion blame for the disaster, finally reached fruition in 1919, when the Appeal Court in London upheld the Canadian Court's ruling that both ships the MONTE-BLANC and IMO were equally to blame a for what occurred to cause the devastating explosion. No individual person(s) were ever indicted. or held to account for what had happened. However the Royal Canadian Navy, still in its infancy, having only been formed in 1910, received severe criticism for the manner in which it had failed in its responsibility to manage the shipping movements within the harbour to a satisfactory level on that fateful day. The impressive Memorial Bell Tower was built at Fort Needham, completed on 9th June,1985, overlooks the explosion site where two churches had once stood. A carillon of ten bells donated by the United Memorial Church hang on the memorial. Annually at 9.00 am on December, 6th, a service is held at the memorial and the bells ring out across 'The Narrows' to commemorate the victims and remind those present of this the worst tragedy in Canadian history.

Wrecked dwellings at Richmond, Halifax. N.S. 1917.

Rail tracks at Halifax. N.S. 1917

Wrecked houses at Dartmouth, Halifax. N.S. 1917.

BETWEEN 40 and 60 DEGREES NORTH.

HOME FOR CHRISTMAS!

The author was a cadet on CAIRNESK. (III) when his older brother Bill Wallace was third mate on CAIRNGOWAN (IV). With both of their ships berthed in Imperial Dock, Leith over Christmas, 1952, this allowed them to spend Christmas 'at home' together, with their parents, for the first time since 1945. It subsequently proved to be the last occasion when everybody was together to celebrate Christmas. A rare event indeed!

This photograph below was taken by an' Edinburgh Evening News' photographer on 24th December, 1952 shows both Cairn Line vessels berthed in Imperial Dock, Leith, along with other ships, as indicated:

1. CAIRNESK (III) – 5,007grt. Cargo/Passenger. Cairn Line of Steamships Ltd.
2. BEN VANNOCH (IV) – (7,069grt). William Thomson, Line. Dundee.
3. CAIRNGOWAN (IV) – (7,503grt) Cargo/Passenger. Cairn Line of Steamships..
4. BENLEDI (IV) – (7884 grt.) in Imperial Dry Dock..Wm. Thomson's Ben Line.
5. MONTE UDALA – (10,170grt.). Cargo/Passenger. Anzar Line. Spain.
6. KARAMU (II) – (1,988grt).New ship by Henry Robb. Leith.(Y/N.426) cargo/passenger. for The Union Steamship Company of New Zealand. The heavy lift crane. on the North side of Imperial Dock is lifting the engine into the hull.

[Imperial Dock, Leith on 24th December, 1952.]

A LESS FORTUNATE SISTER'

The first leg of a voyage would commence with the short trip South from the River Tyne for the River Tees at Middlesbrough, to load cargo and sometimes heavy lifts of machinery usually for power stations in Canada or other steel products from Dorman Longs steelworks at Redcar.

My first voyage in 1950, was on the CAIRNESK (III). She was considered to be an old ship at 24 years of age. She had been built at Sunderland in 1926 along with her sister ship CAIRNGLEN (II) during 'the depression,' by William Pickersgill & Sons, at their Southwick shipyard and was still in a 'well kept' condition. Shortly after clearing the Tyne entrance we headed South for Middlesbrough. As we steamed along the coast one of the crew pointed out a rocky outcrop, known as Camel Island, near Marsden at South Shields. He told me, that it was the wreck site of the CAIRNESK's sister ship, the CAIRNGLEN (II) which had sank there,10 years earlier in 1940, after going aground in thick fog. A new marker buoy had been mistaken for the entrance to the River Tyne and the ship had steamed onto the rocks, broke her back and became a total loss. Fortunately all of the crew were saved. The sinking had happened during war time and the eventual recovery of her desperately needed war cargo of Ford trucks engines, tyres chilled butter and Canadian gammon is purported to have prompted Winston Churchill's famous wartime Parliamentary speech in which he called for everybody to 'Pull together to save the country's bacon' Fame indeed!

CAIRNGLEN(II).Aground at Marsden. October,1940.

HIGH TEES.

On arrival in the Tees we would load cargo either at Middlesbrough Dock or further up stream in the main Channel at the Deep Water Berth next to the famous 'Transporter Bridge'. The two hundred and twenty five foot high structure has been a local landmark since it was constructed in 1911 and can be easily seen as you enter the mouth of the Tees from the sea. It's unique construction allows both vehicular and foot passengers to be carried across the Tees from Middlesbrough town centre to Port Clarence on the rivers North bank in a travelling 'gondola', suspended beneath the bridge on steel wires.

Deck cargo from Middlesbrough, usually for Sorel, would include steel plates, coiled steel wire, dynamos and engines, with return cargoes of grain, flour, aluminium asbestos and fruit.

[Middlesbrough Transporter Bridge.]

Heavy Lift Middlesbrough for Sorel, Canada.

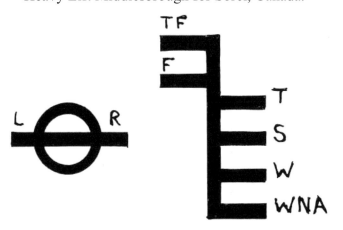

When loading of cargo at Middlesbrough was completed we would leave the Tees for Grangemouth in the Firth of Forth to take on the last of the out bound cargo of either additional steel manufactured goods and other general cargo including cases of whisky. The ship would then be finally battenerd down and steam out into the North Atlantic, via. The Pentland Firth and on to Canada.The average voyage time would be 11 days, depending on the sea conditions and weather, particularly fog and ice in the winter when approaching the Grand Banks and Straits of Belle Isle.

THE OTHER SIDE OF 'THE POND'.: Nova Scotia and The St. Lawrence River.

Port of arrival visited in Canada differed, depended on the winter or summer schedules.

The winter schedule only two ports, St. John. New Brunswick and Halifax N.S. would be visited.

St John: Discharge general cargo and steel products and load, grain, flour timber. Copper and aluminium ingots.

Halifax: Discharge general cargo and steel and load?

Both ports were not visited in the summer schedule apart from an occasional visit to Halifax at the end of the summer season to load huge wooden barrels of apple for discharge at Newcastle.

The Summer schedule saw visits to numerous ports in the Province of Quebec all on the St. Lawrence river, to both discharge and load.

Montreal: Head of navigation on the St. Lawrence River, prior to the opening of The St. Lawrence Seaway in 1956. was the usual first port of call inbound from U.K. Discharged general cargo and manufactured steel goods. Loaded Bulk grain and flour at the elevators.

Travelling East on the St. Lawrence River: the following would usually be visited.

Sorel: Discharge point for heavy lift cargoes, Generators etc. from Teeside & Newcastle.

Three Rivers: Load bulk grain and flour from elevators.

Quebec: Only occasional calls with small amounts of general cargo for discharge and load aluminium ingots.

Saguenay River for Port Alfred. to load aluminium slabs and copper ingots.

Baie Comeau: Occasional visits to load aluminium ingots. This would be the last port of call before departing for the return passage for the U.K. apart from the occasional visit to Halifax N.S. towards the end of the summer season, to load apples for Newcastle. There was no transhipment of cargoes within Canadian waters.

The return voyage to the U.K. usually took 9 days, returning via the Pentland Firth. Leith, my home port, would be the first U.K. port of call to discharge the main bulk of the cargo of grain and flour at the Imperial Docks grain mills.

Leith to Newcastle Quay Side was the final leg in the round trip, to Discharge: General foodstuffs, for the CWS, animal feeds copper ingots and bulk tallow for Thomas Hedleys soap works. Occasionally a trip through the swing bridge to Dunston to discharge a last part cargo of grain and flour at the CWS flour mills at Dunston, would bring to an end the round voyage which would take an average have taken six weeks to complete.

During my time with the Cairn Line I made twenty eight crossings of the North Atlantic to and from Canada and recall some of the more unusual incidents that have remained with me from that time.

Outward Bound.   Inward Bound.
CAIRNESK (III) 1950's.

SMOG ON THE TYNE.

Arriving at the mouth of the Tyne on one occasion, we laid off about one mile waiting for the pilot. There was a sea mist but we could make out the shoreline and the Tyne entrance. Standing on the deck, we saw a black mist in the river mouth. It appeared to get larger and larger. When it reached the mouth of the river, it seemed to dispatch itself from the shoreline and move out into the North Sea. We realised it was 'smog' and in the form of a very enormous ball shape cloud. The wind was slight, but it seemed to propel 'the ball' along and we saw it was approaching in our direction. It started to envelope the CAIRNESK (III), and within five minutes the smog cloud passed over and was last seen heading North East across the North Sea. It was industrial smog, which rises and collects under a low cloud ceiling. The ship was covered in a fine black soot, we all had to hose the ship down from bow to stern.

FORTH.

Sailing into the Firth of Forth, between May Island, and the Bass Rock, the pilot cutter would come from Fidra Isle. The pilot would board the ship by means of a rope ladder on the lee side.

Approaching Leith Docks, with the City of Edinburgh behind, you would see a layer of smoke hanging low over the city. Sea mist and fog would make the situation worse. So from ages gone by, the city was known as "Auld Reekie". Edinburgh is built on seven hills, one called Calton Hill. On top are situated several buildings e.g. an observatory, an obelisk and a tower in the shape of Nelson telescope (upside down). At 1155hrs every day, a black ball is raised on a pulley contraption to a yardman, at the top of this tower. Exactly at 12noon, the ball drops, thus indicating true Greenwich time. The purpose is to inform all officers of ships either at anchor in Leith docks, Firth of Forth or sailing past Edinburgh at noon. In those days, coal was the fuel, so with all the houses and factories, shipyards etc. pouring out their smoke, it would rise and linger just above the city. The hills helped to prevent the smoke from clearing, so it would be a regular sight to see Edinburgh with a layer of smoke hovering.

In 1952 in Leith, Bill Everington and I were up painting the funnel, when the 1st Mate came and informed us that Andrew Guild, our bosun had been killed in a train accident. The 1st Mate knocked us off for the rest of the day. Andrew had been a well liked and respected man.

Rope Ladder.

Bass Rock– Firth of Forth.

Forth Rail Bridge.

From Leith to Grangemouth, we pass under the Forth Rail Bridge.

ROGUE WAVE.

We were about two days out from the Butt of Lewis and the weather was atrocious. The two Seamen were the watch helmsmen and I was the 'farmer' (bridge lookout). I had a 'smoko' at 02.00hrs and returned to the monkey island. The 1st helmsman then went for his break. I was at the front part on the port side of the island. The swell was running from our starboard quarter. As I remember, the weather was classed as a storm Force 12 (up to 80+ m.p.h.) The swell was enormous and what with the waves, it was, "one hell of a night to be out in a ship". The swell would roll under our starboard quarter, move along under the keel and come up forward of this ship. As this motion took place, the ships stern would rise up and the ship would level out on top of the crest (like a sea saw). The bows would rise up, the stern down, whereupon the ship would slide down the back of the swell. By which time, the stern is starting to rise the next swell and the action is repeated again and again. The wave on top of the swell, was in itself heavy, and the wind howling and blowing across the tops of the swell causing the wave scenario rougher. Swells are roughly constant at times, where as waves can create rougher disturbance on top of the swell, and there again the sea can cause very choppy motions. About fifteen minutes later, as I stood huddled in the corner of the island, I happened to look astern, towards our starboard quarter.

The sky and sea appeared to be one, what with the flying spray of sea and the rain and the darkness of the night, but in the distance, maybe 1/8 mile, I saw a long high stretch of white 'foam' on the crest of a wave. There must have been three swell ridges all topped off with white crests, between 'it' and the CAIRNESK (III), but I could see it clearly, as it was higher than the three ridges, we rode the nearest swell, o.k. but I then realised that the 'foamy' wave was in fact a 'rogue' wave. I had heard about such events, but never thought I would experience one so soon. What with the trough between the swell, and the height from that to the crest of this wave was 60 feet plus. Not to forget the turbulent sea action on top of the crest. So you can imagine what we were about to experience. I dashed to the mouth pipe (connecting the monkey island to the wheelhouse) and blew down. The 2nd Mate answered and I shouted there's a hell of a big wave on our starboard quarter".

He shouted "right" and as he answered, this 'rogue wave' enveloped us in a tremendous burst of sea and spray. At the same time, the ship was pitching and rolling. The helmsman did a great job keeping the ship at right angles to the swell. As this passed over, I thought it couldn't get worse. Was I wrong! As I looked to the starboard quarter, this time I saw a 'vast cloud of foam'. This wave was higher than the first rogue wave. At first I stood mesmerised, thinking nothing could be as big and high, in what was happening, but I was wrong.

In my opinion, we didn't fully ride this wave as the stern ploughed through near the top. The vast amount of water that fell on top of us was pushing the ship down into the sea.

The sound was thunderous and for a few seconds, everything appeared 'white' this is the best way I can describe the scene. Then, all I could see on the foredeck was the foremast, the rest was covered in white sea foam, and like being in a 'very large sea bubble bath'. I dashed to the after end of the monkey island, and only saw the funnel and the top of our accommodation.

I started to feel the ship heaving, trying to come up out of the sea. I started to go forward of the 'island' and felt that we were slipping down the back of the rogue wave. I could feel the enormous weight of the sea trying to keep us down. It seemed to last forever, but at last the CAIRNESK (III) started to rise up like the "Phoenix", and the water poured through the scuppers and tumbled over the bulwarks.

As I looked forward, the water then poured through the scuppers and on the forecastle, derrick, cowels and hatches came into sight. I went aft again on the island, and saw the complete boat deck, derricks on No3, 4 and 5 holds and poop had appeared. Once again the helmsman had done a great job in steering the ship. I later found out the water had swept down into the crews quarters, leaving them rather wet. I estimated the whole incident took about 5 to 10 minutes. Apart from being apprehensive, it was exhilarating-talk about your adrenalin flowing. It was certainly a once in a lifetime experience.

Thinking back on the first rogue 60' plus, I estimate that the second rogue was 80' plus the sea turbulence. After the second rogue, believe it or not, the storm appeared to abate slightly. We continued on our way, but not without damage. The starboard davits, lifeboats, along with the starboard side of the bridge, were damaged. Temporary repairs were carried out when we arrived in Halifax and on arriving back in Leith, tradesmen from Henry Robb shipyards were waiting on the quayside, to make permanent repairs to damage. My experience made me think about the mystery of the Flannen Isles, off the Western Isles of Scotland in 1900. When three lighthouse keepers were mysteriously swept to their deaths by 'rogue waves.' and their bodies were never found.

The 'Rouge' Crew, GIL (3rd right) BILL EVERINGTON (4TH right.).

SOUTH SHIELDS & THE DOLE.

About two days out from Leith, I was working with an A.B. at the stern (1200-1600hrs). He suddenly told me he could smell a strong scent of rose flowers. I didn't smell the scent, but didn't doubt him, however we both forgot the incident. On arrival in Leith, 2 days later, the Captain sent for the A.B. and informed him his grandmother had died two days before (later ascertained it was in the afternoon). The A.B., a regular on the CAIRNESK (III) was allowed to go home to Newcastle. Returning after the funeral. "strange things do happen".

In July 1952, the CAIRNESK (IIII) went into dry dock at Middle Docks in South Shields for a refit. All of the crew, and us, the Cadets were 'paid off.' The company was not obliged to keep us on so I signed on the "dole" and on 3rd. November, 1952 I was recalled and signed on in Grangemouth. Before leaving the CAIRNESK (III) in South Shields, I learnt about dry docking and the stresses involved when the water is removed from the dry dock.

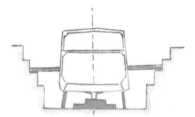

DRY DOCK STRESSES.

BAD WEATHER. One trip in December, 1952,on the CAIRNESK. We were having a rough passage from Montreal for Leith with 6,500 tons of grain and flour. The ship was battered by heavy seas, when water got into No. 2 hold, spoiling part of the cargo. At that time the U.K. was being lashed with severe stormy weather. Winds were being recorded at over 100 mph, not as bad as January, 1953 highest wind recording then was 150 mph.

We heard a Swedish tanker OIJAREN, 8,683grt. went aground on the Muckleskerry, Pentland Firth. All the crew got off, but a week later returned to re-float her. On checking the ship the crew found that some unauthorised persons had come on board. Personal possessions, 50,000 American cigarettes tobacco also instruments and gear had been stolen. Classed as piracy, police and customs were notified and Captain Lottijer was most annoyed to say the least. So much for neutrality and the 'Shetland Bus'.

> ### HAPPY NEW YEAR.
> We were berthed at Jarrow coal Staithes taking on bunkers and preparing to sail for Halifax and St John.
> It was the 31st. December 1952 and at lunch time some crew members went ashore for refreshment .at the near by tavern. No sign of them returning, so the Bosu'n was sent ashore to get them. No sign again, so Bill Everington and I were sent, found them, and tried to get them to go back on board.. Naturally we drank to their health, and then the 3rd Mate appeared, we had one for the road, and we all returned to the ship.I must say, the 1st Mate was reasonable about it all, as it was after all, Hogmanay. Anyway, we soon departed the Tyne and brought in the New Year steaming North past Aberdeen. for The Pentland Firth. The song "The Northern Lights of Old Aberdeen" seemed was very apt.

'FISHY TAIL.'.

Again in 1952 on the CAIRNESK, we passed through the Pentland Firth and turned South round Duncansby Head, with the tide with us, heading for Leith. The tide could in fact add three or four knots to our speed, and passing through the whirlpools, we would sail faster. Anyway, one time we were doing this manoeuvre, we had turned our headdue south when the engines stopped. Being curious, we went out onto the boat deck, in time to see a basket being passed down on our portside to a trawler, which had come alongside. After a few minutes, the basket was retrieved full of fish. The Captain had fancied some fresh fish in return for spirits and cigarettes. 'Smokkies' for 'Smokkies'!

RADIAL DAVITS

BOAT DRILL!

In 1953 one trip to Halifax and St. John, we were about half way across 'the pond' and sailing through a gale. About 03.00hrs on morning, the ships whistle started blowing seven times – 'an emergency'. We attended to our boat stations, I was at the starboard side along with half the crew. The 2nd Mate was in charge and he ordered us to raise the lifeboats and prepare to swing them out. Our lifeboats had radial davits, where you have to raise by block and tackle by pulling on ropes. We got the forward boat raised, but a rope snagged on the outside of the lifeboat. An A.B., a big well seasoned seaman from Newcastle known as "Big Geordie" stepped round the front of the lifeboat to free the rope but just at that moment, the ship lurched to starboard, his feet slipped and Geordie would have been away. He had managed to keep a grip with one hand on the lifeboats gunnel, and the Bosun and I gripped him and pulled him back round the front of the lifeboat to safety on to the boat deck. At this moment the 1st Mate came up the outside steps onto the boat deck. He informed the 2nd Mate to replace the lifeboats in their chocks, as it had all been a practise drill on the Captains instructions. We just stood and looked at each other. The weather was atrocious, and a seaman had nearly lost his life. So when "Big Geordie" heard the 1st Mates remark, he said something like "I'll bloody kill him", and made to go down the stairway intending to go onto the bridge. The mate, Bosun, Bill Everington and I restrained him, whereupon he went off to his cabin. But only after he got the Mates word that he would see to the Captain. Later, I wondered what the consequences would have been if "Big Geordie" had fallen overboard, we couldn't have saved him due to the weather. At this stage, I would like to say that all strange incidents involved the same Captain. Shortly afterwards he took leave but later returned. One time the same Captain appeared at Milburn House in his dressing gown. However, I was informed that when this Captain sailed as Chief Officer, he was very obliging and took time out to instruct the Cadets in seamanship and navigation. In fact, he was a good instructor and an excellent Chief Officer. Strange man!

ICEBERG : (CAIRNESK).

In 1953, I remember one incident regarding an iceberg, we were sailing westwards, weather good, medium swell, with slightly choppy seas. As we sailed along, working on deck, we saw a large iceberg about three miles off on our starboard bow. Some of the passengers were trying to take photographs – we then became aware that the iceberg was straight ahead of the ship. We looked aft and saw the ships wake had altered to starboard. When we were about a mile of the iceberg, the ship turned to port, putting the iceberg again on our starboard midships. The passengers were naturally pleased, they got better photographs of the berg. Personally we thought it was crazy, when we heard the Captain had instructed the helmsman to make these manoeuvres – Apparently not clad in his dressing gown on that occasion. "there's nothing stranger than folk".

COAL TEA.: (CAIRNESK).

This reminds me of a trip to Halifax, which took 19 days. The weather was worse than the "big two" but no "rogues" (thank goodness) but the weather was classed again as a storm. During this lengthy trip, our coal bunkers were thinning out, but normally there is enough coal for approximately 12 days plus, but not 19. As time went on, when the coal in the centre of the hold was finished, the firemen had to shift the coal from the wings, thereby having to carry the coal further. So the deck crew and Cadets took turns and went down to shift the coal from the wings, corners etc. into the centre of the hold. This work is covered in the ships article's. We just made Halifax with not much coal left in the bunkers.

The end of this story, every time a crew member went down for a spell on coming up he would receive a tot of rum, from the Chief Steward. Naturally we went along as well but he said no. We didn't agree with him, so we spoke to the 1st Mate. He took the view, if we work like the deck crew, we should receive the same reward. So we did.

Arthur ARMSTRONG and daughter. 1952.

WHITEWASH.

Going home one time in summer, about four days out from Butt of Lewis in very good weather with a slight swell. Andrew the Bosun decided to have the mast stays painted. The paint is a mixture of thick white wash and grease and is applied on the stay. So Arthur and I were paired off, to do the after stay on the main mast. Arthur thought I should gain the experience. It was my first time. First I shimmed up the topmast with a rope, put it through a single block tackle, and tied it in an overhand knot in case it slipped, just under the 'hounds band', with a shackle.

Went back down with the rope and secured it to the Bosuns chair with a bowline and two half hitches and 'end whipped' to chair rope. Arthur pulled the chair up and put several turns round a winch drum. I went back up with a bucket of paint and cotton waste, to the crosstrees, where I tied the bucket on a railing. Because I had to go back up the top mast and secure the chair to the stay with a second shackle. Collected the paint, tie it to the chair and climb into the chair. As Arthur lowered me slowly down, I swabbed the stay. It was a dirty job but satisfying–after reaching the poop deck.

JOINING SHACKLE.

GHOSTS.

Crossing to the extreme–one trip to Montreal we had quite a smooth crossing. I was on the helm, and there shouldn't be any lights on the fore deck. Steering along I saw a light flickering on and off in the ships hospital, also used as a lock up for troublesome crew. Anyway, I told the 3rd Mate and he looked and also saw the light. The ships hospital is situated on the port bow underneath the fo'c'sle head. The 3rd Mate called up the standby seaman and told him to investigate. On returning, he looked rather bewildered, and explained that on going inside the hospital, which only contained a bed and chair, nothing else, he saw there was no bulb in the light socket and the light switch was broken. The seaman checked the rest of the focsle head but found nothing untoward. The light never came on again!

BEFORE THE MAST.

Later on the same ship, we were sailing up the St Lawrence, in coldly frosty weather, I think past Sorel, when a rain cloud came down the river towards us and enveloped the ship. It was like a wall of water! It lasted about 5 minutes, when suddenly there was a tremendous crack. As we were in our mess room, we looked aft out of the portholes and saw a Ball running along the ships ariel (some call it a fireball). There was a bright flash then another crack and we saw the top of the main mast with the truck, break off (about 4 feet). I was on the 1st Mates watch, so I had to climb the mast and inspect for any more damage. I saw there was a split of about 6 feet in length, but the hounds band had held it together. We got a new top mast when we arrived back in Newcastle.

SEEING THE LIGHTS.

Another trip sailing Eastwards for the UK, we were at the Northern part of our intended course, in cold and frosty weather when I experienced my first sight of the 'Aurora Borealis', it was fantastic. I did see it again two or three times in my four years–but in different colours, yellow to red. How I wished I carried a camera with me to capture all, of the strange colours.

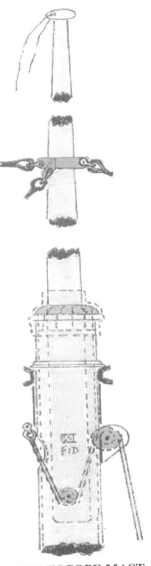

TELESCOPE MAST

ARTIST'S LICENCE

Aurora Borealis.

One time the CAIRNESK (III) was at the quayside and riggers were going to move the ship up river to Dunston. We were going to discharge the rest of our grain cargo. I was on the helm, the other Cadets were on leave. The pilot was also on the bridge, when the Captain appeared. Prior to this move, the topmasts had been lowered into the telescopic lower mast, necessary for moving up river. I heard the pilot speaking to the Captain, then he spoke to me (the pilot I had met on several occasions). He told me to follow his instructions, as the Captain had final responsibility I looked to him, whereupon I realised the Captain did not look well (he had just returned after having been off the previous trip). Anyway, our trip up river to Dunston was uneventful, and two days later, we moved back down to the quayside.

One of our 'dangerous' cargoes, although at the time we were ignorant of the danger to our health, was asbestos-white and blue variants, packed into paper bags and loaded in Quebec for Newcastle (approx 1000 tons) and Leith (100 tons). One place asbestos was mined, in a north district of N.F. and shipped to Quebec. The asbestos to Newcastle was for Armstrong Cork Co. Team Valley Estate, who manufactured vinyl and cork tiles. The bags would burst and the asbestos dust would 'fly' around when loading/discharging. No masks or special clothing then, not like now, trained specialist teams would have to be appointed to deal with asbestos. Several persons involved in the transport/handling of asbestos, would be affected later on in life. Most people would take longer to be affected by the dust. I know a retired police colleague who died recently at the age of 80, who had served in the Royal Navy as a stoker, during WWII. Cause of death ASBESTOSIS. A few months later, I had occasion to go to Milburn House, speaking to the Personnel Manager. As we talked, I asked if I could transfer to the CAIRNGOWAN (IV) having one year left, before going ashore (2nd Mate). He agreed, so in early 1954, I joined the CAIRNGOWAN (IV) in Leith Docks. Being a new ship, the conditions were excellent, especially the accommodation, sharing a cabin with Cadet David Curry. Dining was in the Officers Mess (uniform).

CHAPTER 6

SAME COMPANY - NEW SHIP : CAIRNGOWAN(IV).

CAIRNGOWAN(IV).

'CHALK & CHEESE.'

I left the CAIRNESK in December,1952, and joined the CAIRNGOWAN(IV) as a Cadet, on 23rd January, 1954, at Leith docks. In service for only two years, she was a relatively new ship. Along with her sister-ship the CAIRNDHU(IV), she was the product of West Hartlepool shipbuilders, William Gray & Company Ltd. Both completed in 1952, they were also turbine steamers, but unlike the CAIRNESK(III), they were oil fired, so no more taking on coal bunkers and the dirt. There was a stark contrast between the two ships, The CAIRNGOWAN, with all of her 'mod cons.' and the old reliable CAIRNESK, with all of the dents, scrapes and maladies, associated with her 28 years of arduous service on the North Atlantic.

When I joined the CAIRNGOWAN (IV) the following personnel were part of the crew:

CAPTAIN Ian Grant FOSTER	Master.
J. POTTER	Chief Officer.
J.LOBBAN	2nd Mate.
A. STANTON	3rd. Mate.
D. CURRY	Cadet.
K. HUNTER	Cadet.
B. W. PICKERING	Cadet.
W. S. WILKINSON.	Chief Engineer.
E. JOHNSON	Radio Officer.
J. CORFIELD	Radio Officer. (Trainee.)
J.CAVANAGH	Chief Steward.
H.WATSON	1st. Steward.
J. BELL	Boatswain.

During my last voyage on the CAIRNGOWAN (IV), we put in to St John's N.F. the anchorage is a natural harbour with wharves on the north side. The entrance to the harbour is called 'The Narrows.' There is a Fort-Amherst on the South cliff top, and the North hilltop, was known as 'Signal Hill.'

We were to berth near to the Queens Battery, on the North side. I was the helmsman and as we passed through 'the Narrows', we came upon a marvellous panoramic sight. The harbour was congested and full of mostly sailing ships. There were three factory ships (approximately 3,000grt.) and other distant -water steam trawlers, along with numerous smaller fishing vessels all lying together within the inner harbour.

The sailing ships consisted of all types: e.g. three and four masted square rigged, sloops, schooners, barques, some ketches, and barquentines etc.

POLEMAST SCHOONER   FORE-&-AFT SCHOONER

BARQUENTINE   BARQUE

SCHOONER KETCH   SHIP

The ships were mostly Portuguese, but there were a few other nationalities. They were all preparing to start fishing on the Grand Banks, South of Newfoundland. "COD WAS GOD". The next day, I walked up 'Signal Hill' to Cabot Tower', however, most of the ships had sailed the previous evening. I photographed the panoramic view of the bay, using up three frames from my Brownie box camera. It shows five deep-sea trawlers and three squared rigged sailing ships, one berthed below the stern of CAIRNGOWAN(IV).

Signal Hill: CAIRNGOWAN(IV) berthed near the Queens Battery on the North side. on 7th September,1954.

Panoramic view of harbour from Signal Hill.

This is a fine example of a 4 masted schooners, I saw in St Johns N.F. in 1954.(David R. Macgregor).

The Author has a model of a Hermaphrodite Brig. It is made from scrap metal by a Clifford Scupham, master blacksmith of Portobello. He has created many such models.

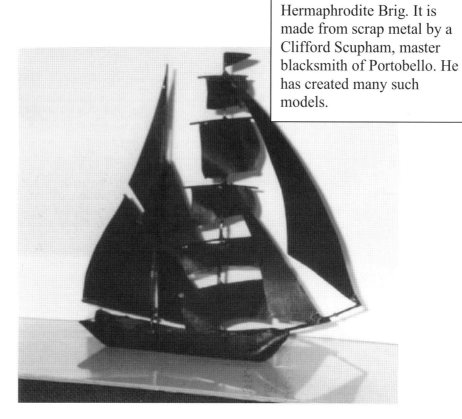

SIGNAL HILL N.F. TO PORTOBELLO.

On 2 June 1896, Guqlielmo Marconi (1874-1937) took a patent out for the first wireless telegraph. In 1901 Marconi transmitted and received signals between Cornwall UK and Newfoundland (Signal Hill). It was Signal Hill that the transmission was carried out, later in 1909 Marconi was awarded a Nobel prize for physics.

HE BEAT MARCONI TO IT

A Scot who rarely received credit for his pioneer efforts in radio has died in England at 76, and his death has brought to light a story of wireless experiments at Portobello, Edinburgh, as early as 1909. Had Mr Andrew Burns been given co-operation by the Government he could perhaps have been recognised throughout the world as a man of equal importance to Marconi. He can safely be called one of the pioneers of wireless telephony.

Born in 1887, Mr Burns was the son of an Edinburgh dental surgeon who practiced in London but later returned to Scotland. It was in Portobello that Mr Burns, as a youth of 18, began transmitting and receiving voices over the air.

Achievements

This was in 1905. Four years later he demonstrated his achievements at Portobello Pier on the Firth of Forth. Reporters and scientists from all parts of Britain flocked to the pier to wonder at this "marvellous invention."

"Wireless telephony had been successfully demonstrated," they explained to all the world.

One newspaper described Mr Burns's accomplishments in this way: "Mr Andrew Burns, after several years of persistent, painstaking and patient study, carried on with indomitable will and confident convictions as to the final results, has successfully solved the problem of wireless telephony and has given a practical demonstration of its faultless achievement on the Portobello Pier."

Andrew Burns

Shortly afterwards, Mr Burns founded a wireless school on Portobello Pier to train others in the use of his equipment.

Then came World War I.

While Mr Burns was away on his honeymoon, the War Office closed down his station under the Official Secrets Act. Had his work occurred just before World War II, the Government would have probably assisted him; but the Government's close-down practically dealt a death-blow to Mr Burns's spirit.

"My father's whole career was buried by this blow," said his son, Mr Andrew Burns, jun. "This action so upset him that he rarely spoke about his invention afterwards. He was a modest man, but now I think the truth should be known."

But for the Government's action, the son explained, Mr Burns might have become a multi-millionaire.

He tried to join the Navy, then the Army, to try to further his work; but both Services turned him down on medical grounds. Eventually he joined the L.M.S. Railway in London as a sub-station attendant, from which he was retired at age 65.

Now he is dead, and his story is the tragedy of a little-known genius.

NEWSPAPER ARTICLES

MR ANDREW BURNS" – who pioneered in wireless transmission on the pier at Portobello – met his wife when she was on holiday at Joppa in Edinburgh. In a letter to the "Weekly Scotsman" from his home in Tadworth, Surrey, Mr Andrew Burns jun. Explained: "He was, my mother told me, a wonderful teacher – a man who was full of patience and easy to understand...His interest in electrical matters never dimmed, and only a few months ago he was hoping to get an electrical article published". Perhaps like another Scottish genius named Burns, he will now be appreciated far more – after he is gone.

A FEW DAYS LATER ANOTHER NEWSPAPER WROTE:

"The information the other day circulated through the London Press that a certain gentleman was the first inventor of a system of wireless telephony to carry the voice over space and through concrete material, came as quite a surprise in scientific circles in Scotland, because as a matter of fact...an able and accomplished young electrician in the person of Mr Andrew Burns had already invented a system".

The picture showing "budding footballers" were crew members of the CAIRNGOWAN (IV) in 1955. On trips to Canada and New Zealand, they would organise matches with local football clubs or teams from other visiting ships.

CAIRNGOWAN (IV) FOOTBALL TEAM : 1955

Back Row; Captain Foster (manager), Cook, Chief cook. Unknown, unknown, A Stanton, J. Cavanagh (coach)
Front Row; Unknown, N. Hindmarsh, Unknown, H. Watson, Unknown, H. Millar.

'CAIRNGOWAN.' 3.   —-   **'MANCHESTER CITY' 1.**

"Our coach was the chief steward and our self-appointed manager the ship's master, Captain Foster of Newcastle – an extremely nice man who was a Newcastle United "nut".

I vividly recall the time when Newcastle beat Manchester City in the FA Cup Final in 1955. We were due to leave Montreal and several of us were huddled around a radio listening to the match, including Capt. Foster. He refused to sail until the final whistle had blown – much to the disgust of the French-Canadian pilot.

As we pulled away and were being taken to the main channel by tugs, the first ship we passed was the MANCHESTER CITY, one of the many operating Manchester Liners Shipping Co.

The galley crew, good humouredly, came out banging pots and pans, cheering us – much different to what would happen today. I can remember all the faces in the photo, but, alas, most of the names have deserted me.

Neil Hindmarsh. 3rd Engineer
NEWCASTLE EVENING CHRONICLE

The CAIRNGOWAN (IV) sailed back to the UK berthing in Leith Docks on 16 September 1954, where I 'signed off.' for the final time.

During my short time at sea, I had made 28 crossings of the Atlantic Ocean, 22 on the CAIRNESK (III) and 6 on the CAIRNGOWAN (IV). I sailed under five different Captains, who were all gentlemen and served with hundreds of fellow crewmembers.

Thereafter I attended Leith Nautical College for approximately 2 months, however because of personal and family reasons, I decided to 'leave the sea' and I volunteered for the Royal Air Force (Provost) Police serving for three years.

THE QUEENS SHILLING.

During 1956 whilst serving in RAF (Provost) Police, I spent four days on board the troopship EMPIRE ORWELL in Southampton. I was with 215 wing, comprising of 250 R.A.F personnel and 1000 Household Guards, waiting to sail for the Suez Canal Zone. However, the Prime Minister, Sir Anthony Eden, resigned, thus we were returned to units (RAF Yatesbury).

Voyage No. 29. cancelled by the kind intervention of 'Uncle Sam.'

EMPIRE ORWELL.

QUEEN ELIZABETH 2.

In 1993 my wife and I sailed our first cruise as passengers on the Cunard liner QUEEN ELIZABETH. 2. The year previous, in the August of 1992, she had grounded at Cuttyhunk Island, near Cape Cod while on a cruise to Halifax, Nova Scotia an area I had sailed on numerous occasions with the Cairn Line. She was fortunately refloated, repaired and put back into service, in good time for us to enjoy our cruise. During my time with the Cairn Line I regularly departed and arrived in the River Tyne at all hours of the day and night on our trips to Canada and it was always a most impressive sight.

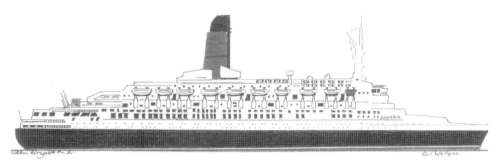

QUEEN ELIZABETH 2

During Sepember, 2007, I was pleased to hear that the 'Q.E.2' had 'called in' on the Tyne for the first and only time in its career, as part of her farewell cruise around the U.K. prior to her retirement in 2008.

[Bulletfoto]

The R.M.S. QUEEN ELIZABETH 2. is shown entering the River Tyne on 16th of September, 2007, shrouded in smoke and fireworks, from pyrotechnics displays on both piers, afforded to her, as remarkably, she was making her first ever visit to the river in her 38 years history. Recently sold for use as a floating hotel and conference centre at the worlds largest man-made island, The Palm Jumeirah Island Complex, at Dubai, in the United Arab Emirates she is the first of many passenger vessels to be prematurely forced out of service by the impending 'Solas 2010' regulations on passenger ship construction and safety, which will ultimately foreshorten the service of many of today's liners. Currently holding the record as Cunards longest serving ship, (previously held by R.M.S.AQUITANIA's 35 years), her final voyage is scheduled to depart Southampton for Dubai on 11th November, 2008.

CHAPTER. 7.

CAREER HISTORIES: A correlation of Seafarers 'Tales' who have, at some time, in their careers, served with The Cairn Line of Steamships.

(7a). **John Oliver BAND** - Master Mariner.

'CAIRNISLA' 24.1.1902.

John Oliver Band was born on 24th December 1868 in Derby and between 1881 and 1882 he immigrated to Massachusetts, in the U.S.A. the voyage was from Liverpool to Boston. His first job was a 'printers devil' (office boy/apprentice) but moved on when 15 years old and purchased a horse and cart. He would go to Boston Docks and purchase any useful items he thought he could sell to dealers or tradesmen. He was a general carrier of goods. Later he sold up and became, a 'hobo'(tramp) and travelled around the country for nearly two years. John returned to Boston and decided to go to sea.

In 1885 he joined a 'square rigger' on a regular run from Boston to San Francisco, the cargo out was salt and back with hides. He made two round trips via. the Cape Horn, one trip was called 'checkerboard' because one watch was white crew and the other watch was black crew. One trip John fell from the rigging onto the deck with no apparent injuries. Had he fallen into the sea, that would have been his 'lot', as the ship couldn't or maybe wouldn't have turned round to pick him up. John later sailed on both American and British ships, claiming 'good food' on the 'Yankee' and 'not so good' on the 'British'. On one ship John thought it was in poor condition, and therefore asked the Captain if he could 'sign off' in Bombay. The Captain refused his request, but John decided to go 'jump ship' which turned out to be a very wise move, as later the ship was lost with all hands. It was not known if John had been an apprentice or an Ordinary Seaman, but he acquired navigational skills and rose through the ranks in a very short time.

In 1892, the Cairn Line of Steamships Co. Ltd. was formed. In 1893 at the age of 24, John returned to the UK and served as an able bodied seaman on the CROWN PRINCE, the voyage lasting seven months. In his discharge book, No 3424, issued at Cardiff, it showed he served as 2nd Mate on the S.W. KELLY between 20 August 1893 and 17 January 1894, and he made four trips in the same capacity.

John then joined the MERCIA on the 7th June 1895 as 2nd Mate and was promoted to 1ST Mate on 11th September 1896. He left the MERCIA on 18th July 1897 to study and later he was examined for his 'Certificate of Competency' as Master of a foreign-going ship', which was awarded on 21st August, 1897 at South Shields. On this date John was now 28 years and 8 months old. His next ship was the STRAITS OF MAGELLAN and now armed with his 'Masters Ticket' he was appointed Chief Mate, and duly made two short voyages.

On 22nd February 1898, John joined the CAIRNLOCH as Chief Mate. After two voyages, on the CAIRNLOCH he was given his first command, the CAIRNGLEN (I) at the age of 30 years. On 24th January 1902, Captain Band took command of a new ship the steamer CAIRNISLA. built by Short Bros. Ltd. of Sunderland. As his children were growing up, Captain Band would take them with him on the CAIRNISLA on voyages to Canada, visiting Quebec, 'Trois Rivieres' and Montreal. One time on their way to Quebec, they saw the Chateau Frontenac Hotel on fire. They also visited the Montmorency Falls, the highest waterfall in Canada (East of Quebec City). Captain Band then became Master of the CAIRNTORR(I) a Turret deck steamer built by William. Doxford & Sons at Sunderland in 1904, the only 'Turret deck steamer to be' owned by the Cairn Line.

In 1911, Captain Band again took his children on the CAIRNTORR(I), from Middlesbrough to Quebec and Montreal. The next trip in the CAIRNTORR (I) was to Venice, where their cargo of 8000 tons of coal was unloaded by hand basket in a week. They left in ballast for the Black Sea and proceeded to Odessa for orders, which were to sail to Nicolia, some 150 miles up the Crimean Coast, to load wheat. The CAIRNTORR (I) then sailed to Rotterdam, unloaded and then sailed to Middlesbrough to load iron ore for Canada.

Captain Band was expected 'to found' the ship, this meant that he received a fixed sum to feed his crew. Captain Band was a great believer in feeding his men well. One time, on a Crimean trip he went with the Black cook to purchase the food, whereupon they purchased sheep, 24 geese and some ducks. A pen was constructed on the deck to hold the sheep, and the policy of feeding the crew properly was well rewarded, as men would wait to sign on to his ships.
As Captain Band continued with his career with the Cairn Line of Steamships, and as Master of the CAIRNISLA, he distinguished himself in a well documented Atlantic Ocean rescue of a ships crew.
On 27th. February 1904, a Canadian Barque MARY A. TROOP on passage from Pensacola for Rio de Janeiro, was dismasted in Mid-Atlantic and the crew abandoned all hope. This incident resulted in great publicity in the British press.
Accordingly Captain BANDS 'home town' newspapers, the 'Belper News' and 'Derbyshire Telegraph' carried the following article

'JOHN OLIVER BAND. Master Mariner.'

"Native of Derby, of the CAIRNISLA, Newcastle., who gallantly saved a crew of thirteen lives, 2nd. March,1904, from the barque, MARY A. TROOP. The MARY A. TROOP had been twenty five days a wreck, and for nine days the crew had neither food nor water. They ate wood and chewed lead to appease hunger and thirst. "

This event resulted in the Canadian Government presenting Captain Band with a large silver cup and the owners of the MARY A TROOP commissioning a Canadian artist to paint a large picture of the artists impression of the rescue. In addition the Cairn Line presented him with watch, fob and chain, suitably inscribed, to mark his achievement.

CAIRNISLA.

JOHN BAND

In 1916 during the 'ill fated' Gallipoli campaign, he was Master of CAIRNGOWAN (II) trading in the Mediterranean, on a lucrative Government charter, transporting military supplies to the troops.

In 1918, Captain Band was posted to serve with the Eastern Mediterranean Naval Headquarters based in Port Said, by which time he was promoted to Lieutenant Commander, Acting Commander R.N.R. In Egypt he became 'temporary' Captain R.N.R. an almost unheard of appointment for a Reserve Officer. He was responsible for Naval Transport in the Eastern Mediterranean, including coaling, which was then a crucial commodity of supply carried by the 'fleet train' to the numerous Royal Navy outlying coaling stations in and around the the Middle East.

By the end of the 1920's, it was obvious that the anticipation of a long post-war boom in industry, had not materialised and ship owners, along with other industrialists, were cutting back. Ships were laid up and crews paid off, in efforts to reduce running costs, in order to deal with the world wide trade slump, of the early 1920's. Captain Band was unwilling to accept the use of the much cheaper option of 'Lascar Crews '(Indian sailors.) favoured by many ship owners, as he had 'more faith in the British crews'. This approach proved to be his down fall and the end of Captain John Oliver Bands maritime career. At 52years of age, disgruntled and believing that the conclusion of the war had been outrageously mishandled by the politicians, he regrettably, retired from the Merchant Navy.

In 1921, he began farming land in Staffordshire. An ignominious end to an outstanding maritime career.

WAR MEDALS AND COMMENDATIONS
JOHN OLIVER BAND
MASTER MARINER
1904 CANADIAN GOVT. COMMENDATION - FOR BRAVERY IN RESCUING CREW OF SINKING SHIP "MARY A TROOP" - AWARDED SILVER 1914-1915 STAR BRITISH WAR MEDAL WWI VICTORY MEDAL 1918

(7b). **Joseph COOK** - Master Mariner.

Joseph COOK.   NO. 022090

The following was researched by his granddaughter Mrs Doreen Morris:

My grandfather Joseph Cook was born in 1868 in Sunderland. He was the second son of a family of six sons, and three daughters, born to Joseph Cook 1833-1915 and Mary (nee Cornforth.). He grew up in a Ship Chandlers Shop, signing on as an apprentice in 1885, with Wm. Nicol and Co. of Liverpool. The apprenticeship was registered at Sunderland.

His first ship was the PER ARDUA.63347 of Liverpool, on a foreign journey to Antwerp, and his first wage was 15 shillings and 9 pence. By 1893, his apprenticeship was completed and he had spent 7 years 4 months and 16 days at sea. He passed his exams at South Shields as Master 022090 in May 1893 and in December 1894 he married Emma Agnes Richmond, the daughter of Samuel Arthur Richmond (M.M). and Emma Elizabeth (nee Constable). They were both born in Essex, and had married in Rotherhithe, Surrey in 1863, before moving to the North East of England. Joseph is first noted as Master of the MARCHIONESS 90305, owned by Taylor Sanderson, of Sunderland, in 1898. This was the third foreign journey on this ship.

He had served on 14 different ships before he signed on the CAIRNBAHN-104297, in March 1907, as 1st Mate under Captain L Johnson. He finished on this ship in October 1912. He became Master on the CAIRNISLA in October 1912 to June 1917.

In October 1913 the CAIRNISLA left Manchester for St Vincent via Cardiff and foreign trade. Left Cardiff 16th December arrived St Vincent 1 January 1914, left Rufisque Africa 15th January left Bordeaux 4 February, arrived Newport 7 February (several men deserted at Cardiff).

The vessel left Newport 12th February, left Marseilles 8th March, Dakar 26th March, Rufisque 29th March, Bathurst 1st April, Kounthow 1st April, Bathurst 10th April, Rusfisque 12th April, Konlock 16th April, Rufisque 22nd April, Dakar 22nd April, Rotterdam 11th May, arrived at Dunston on the Tyne 13th May (Dunston is now a suburb of Gateshead).

On 16th May 1914 the CAIRNISLA left Dunston, for las Palmas 30th May, Rufisque 15th June, Rotterdam 9th July, arrived South Shields 10th July.

I was told that at this point my grandmother and her daughter (my mother, Florence) went home to Sunderland. My Uncle Stanley was born there on 26th July 1914 .

The CAIRNISLA journeys continued and left the Tyne 14th July, Bordeaux 24th July, arrived Berry 28th July (Berry Head near Brixham in Devon).

Later on that year, Captain Joseph Cook living at 124 Cairo Street, Sunderland ACTED WITH CONSPICUOUS BRAVERY IN ENTERING A MINEFIELD NEAR ANTWERP AND ATTEMPTING TO SAVE THE STEAMSHIP ARDMOUNT OF GLASGOW. This vessel, which had a cargo of grain, was proceeding towards England, and she struck two mines in quick succession and made water. The crew took to the boats, but afterwards returned to tow ARDMOUNT, but she struck a third mine. The CAIRNISLA, which carried coal from the Tyne for Antwerp, came on the scene and voluntarily pierced into the minefield, where she stayed for six hours until the ARDMOUNT sank. Captain Cook had boarded the ARDMOUNT and remained for over an hour trying to arrange for it to be towed, all the crew of the ARDMOUNT were saved.

My Grandfather, Captain Joseph Cook's action was brought to the attention of the Board of Trade, and they awarded him a piece of exquisite silver plate, inscribed "in acknowledgement of his services in standing by the ARDMOUNT".

Joseph Cook had served on the WEST MARSH (LATE CAIRNISLA) 14th September 1915 and 10th January 1916, reported to be grounded Whitby Rock, refloated (foundered of the Dardenells September 1957).

Joseph Cook - CAIRNAVON -113657- also served on this ship 1914-1915 then transferred to the CAIRNISLA for a foreign trip, and came off the renamed WEST MARSH on 21st May 1917.

Unfortunately all the papers for this period were destroyed during the London Blitz. My grandfather died in 1938.

November 1917, the S.S. LAMPADA registered London, of which Joseph Cook was Master was torpedoed 3m N. of Whitby. The ship was sunk and the crew left in the boats. The Masters boat was swamped and capsized. Two men got on to the upturned keel but five other drowned. The Master was in the sea for half an hour before he was picked up and taken to hospital. No Hospital record survives in Whitby.

**WAR MEDALS AND COMMENDATIONS
JOSEPH COOK
MASTER MARINER**

**1914 - 1915 STAR
BRITISH WAR MEDAL WWI
VICTORY MEDAL 1918**

(7c). **Douglas Knox CRAWFORD** - Master Mariner.

Douglas Knox Crawford was born on 26th March 1893 at Douglas, Isle of Man. On 18th November 1908 in Leith, Scotland, Douglas signed an ordinary apprentice's indenture (Scotland) with Wm. Thomson & Co., Leith of the "Ben" Line Steamers, for a period of four years.

His apprenticeship was served entirely on the BENLARIG (II) up until 18th November 1912. The BENLARIG (II) 3,921/1904, O.N.118695, built by Bartram & Son, Sunderland, (Yard No. 192). In April 1914 the BENLARIG(II) was acquired by the Royal Navy as a collier No. 617.

[Note: on 2nd April 1917 the BENLARIG (II) whilst on a voyage from Freemantle to Colombo, Ceylon, went missing in the Indian Ocean-nothing found-believed possible sabotage.]

The attached endorsements show Douglas's wages for four years (not a lot!!). The termination of his apprenticeship was signed by A. Wallace, Master of BENLARIG (II).

On 25th February 1913, Douglas signed on the BARON MINTO. (4,537/08) of H Hogarth & Sons, Glasgow, as 3rd Mate. Between 18th November 1913 and 4th June 1914, he served as 2nd Mate (3 voyages) on the ORKLA (2,070/1888,) of Christian Salvesen & Co. of Leith. He then moved to the Cairn Thomson Shipping Company, which had been formed in 1908 between the Cairn Line of Steamships and the Thomson Line of Dundee. Douglas joined the DEVONA(3,779/08) as 3rd Mate (2 voyages) and 2nd Mate (1 voyage) on the JACONA (2,969/08) up until January 1915. At this time the Cairn Thomson had a fleet of 17 ships.

Douglas received two recommendations for his tours of duty, on the DEVONA and JACONA, singed by the Masters D. Murray and J. Neave respectively. At this stage he then sat and attained his 1st Mate certificate.

On 2nd April 1915, Douglas applied and was accepted to serve in the Royal Naval Reserve, with a commission as a Sub Lieutenant. On 26th August, 1916, he attained his Masters Certificate of Competency. Douglas completed tours of duty on several H.M.S Stations, namely, VICTORY(II) - shore base, AMETHYST (II) and (III), converted yachts used as supply depots. In January 1917 he applied and joined the Royal Navy Submarines, serving as Lieutenant onboard the submarine. E48. One of only 262 R.N.R. Officers to serve in submarines in WWI. Throughout this time, E48 would call at HMS BONAVENTURE, CORMORANT, DOLPHIN, MAIDSTONE, VICTORY 2 and VULCAN, for supplies, stores, ammunition, equipment etc. During the latter part of WWI the BONAVENTURE and CORMORANT were stationed in Gibraltar, from where E48 was based.

Later from 7th May 1918, Douglas was an instructor in signalling and gunnery at H.M.S GANGES (II), until 15th January 1920, when he left and rejoined the Merchant Navy. Sailing as 5th Mate onboard PERSIC (11,973/1899), White Star Line (Oceanic Steam Navigation Co), until 2nd September 1923. He continued serving with the White Star Line until 11th December 1928 on the following ships:
IONIC 12,232/1902. 5th Mate - 4 voyages
CEDRIC   21,035/1903.   5th Mate - 3 voyages
BALTIC   23,876/1904.   5th Mate - 7 voyages
CERAMIC   18,481/1913.   3rd Mate - 1 voyage
CELTIC (II)   8,327/1921,   4th Mate - 6 voyages

Note: on 10th December 1928 the CELTIC (II) (American Flag) while attempting to enter Cobh Harbour, Ireland, was driven towards 'Roche's Point', near the entrance and despite attempts to go astern, went aground on the 'Cow and Calfs Rocks'. Within days the two funnels had to be cut to deck level, as they obstructed 'Roches Point' Light. It took 5 years to demolish the wreck insitu. Douglas was aboard at the time but not on watch.

Following the loss of the CELTIC (II), Douglas sailed as 5th Mate on the R.M.S. OLYMPIC (46,359/11), of the White Star Line. Until her last transatlantic voyage in September 1931. She was broken in 1935 by Palmers, at Jarrow, after the yards winding up by the Government National Shipbuilders Security Ltd.

Thereafter due to the depression, like may other seafarers, Douglas accepted "any jobs that were going". He was a salvage officer for Trinity House, concerning of wrecks in the Irish Sea.

In 1935 Douglas was employed by London and North Western Railway - later named London Midland Scottish Railway. They had a fleet of ships based in Holyhead, sailing to/from Dun Laghair and Greenore. The company moved their crews between ships as required and Doulgas served as deck officer on the ships in the following lists, being appointed Master of the last two, much of the trade was Holyhead/Greenore shipping cattle and horses.

SLIEVE BAWNE (II)	1,447/37.	D.O.	B.U. 1972
SLIEVE BLOOM (II)	1,279/30.	D.O.	B.U. 1965
SLIEVE DONARD (II)	1,116/22.	1ST MATE	B.U. 1954
SLIEVE GALLION	1,166/08.	D.O.	B.U. 1937
SLIEVE LEAGUE	1,343/35.	MASTER	B.U. 1967
SLIEVE MORE	1,409/32.	MASTER	B.U. 1965

Still with L.M.& S.R. at Dublin, he sailed on a further two ships, namely CAMBRIA (3,445/21.) as 2nd Mate - 3 voyages, and 1st Mate 1 voyage. His Captain when on the CAMBRIA was Captain William Henry Hughet D.S.C. - a hero of the SCOTIA - lost at Dunkirk on 1st June, 1940. Later he sailed on the HIBERNIA (3,458/20) 2nd Mate - 1 voyage. Unfortunately at this time, Douglas was discharged from the Merchant Navy due to ill health.

WAR MEDALS AND COMMENDATIONS
DOUGLAS KNOX-CRAWFORD
MASTER MARINER

1914 TO 1915 STAR
BRITISH WAR MEDAL WWI
VICTORY MEDAL 1918
MERCANTILE MARINE MEDAL WWI (AWARDED BY BOARD OF TRADE TO MERCHANT NAVY PERSONNEL FOR SERVICE OF ONE OR MORE VOYAGE IN A WAR OR DANGER ZONE)

Note: In reference to medals: **(1)** 1914-15 Star **(2)** British War Medal WWI **(3)** Victory Medal 1918, these were nicknamed 'Pip, Squeak and Wilfred. respectively. In 1919 when medals were being struck and awarded, the Daily Mirror issued a cartoon on 12 May 1919 depicting a story about a dog, penguin and rabbit (medals, 1, 2 & 3 were duly nicknamed). The author was B. J. Lamb and the artist was A. B. Payne.

(7d). **Fred WILKINSON FAIRLEY** - Master Mariner.

Fred Wilkinson Fairley was born at Chester- Le- Street, County Durham, on 21st August 1897.

At the age of 16 years he went to sea as an Apprentice with Walter Runciman's Newcastle based shipping Company, the Moor Line Ltd., and during his four years of apprenticeship he served on their S.S. HAZELMOOR and S.S. FORESTMOOR.

He passed his examinations for 2nd Mate in 1917, Mate in 1919 and Master in 1923. Between 1917 and 1920 he served on the following ships in the capacity as 3rd and 2nd Mate, AVESSAC, THERMIDOR, WAR SETTER and RENFREW.

In 1921 he joined the Cairn Line's SCATWELL as 2nd Officer and was to serve in that company for the remainder of his sea going career.

In 1929 he took command of the S.S. CAIRNGOWAN (III) and on this first voyage the rudder post fractured in heavy weather and the rudder was lost. Unable to steer, a jury rudder was constructed and the voyage was resumed until field ice off Newfoundland prevented further progress. The vessel was eventually towed the last few miles into the port of St John's Newfoundland.

Four images of CAIRNGOWAN(III) taken after losing her rudder in the North Atlantic in March, 1929, and successfully brought into St. Johns. N.F. 'against the odds', by Captain Fairley and her crew. Note damage and fractures to the stern frame and rudder post (below).

Rigging 'Jury Rudder' over side.

CAIRNGOWAN entering 'The Narrows' St. Johns. N.F.
on 9th. March, 1929, towed by the Dutch tug. HUMBER.

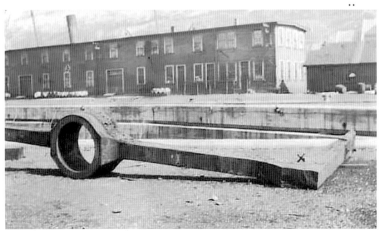
CAIRNGOWAN'S fractured stern frame. at St. Johns N.F.
Taken on 20th April.1929. (Cross marks fracture).

The 1930's was a period of world depression when 12% of the world's merchant ships were laid up. Only three of the Cairn Line's ships continued to trade. As a junior Master Fred reverted to Chief Officer of S.S. CAIRNGLEN (II), the newest ship in the fleet, taking command when trade picked up again, shortly before the outbreak of WW.II.

When war commenced on 3rd September, 1939, he was in command of S.S. CAIRNMONA(II). In October she joined convoy HX.5B together with CAIRNGLEN (II) and CAIRNVALONA on passage from Halifax to the UK. The three ships broke away from the main convoy nearing the British coast to continue their voyage independently to Leith and the Tyne. On the 30th October the CAIRNMONA (II) was torpedoed and sunk by U.13 about three miles off Rattray Head. Three members of the crew were killed by the blast but the remainder were picked up by a fishing boat and landed in Peterhead.

Survivors of the crew of the torpedoed steamer, CAIRNMONA at Peterhead after their rescue in October,1939. (Captain Fairley./second row. 3rd from right. side view).

In the summer of 1940, he took command of the M.V. EMPIRE SAILOR. Formerly CELLINA an Italian motor ship captured at Gibraltar when Italy entered the war. The ship was brought to London in the July and remained there with a part crew throughout the Blitz when 16,000 civilians were killed.

On her first voyage from the Tyne and Grangemouth to Canadian April, 1941, she was attacked by a Focke Wolfe bomber off the North West coast of Scotland. Three bombs caused extensive damage forcing her to return to the Clyde for repairs.

On her 8th voyage across the Atlantic, she was torpedoed by U-518 whilst in convoy ON.145. All but 3 of the 63 persons on board were picked up two Canadian escorts, but a further 20 men died within a few hours as a result of inhaling phosgene gas which had escaped from the cargo hold, when the vessel was hit. Late in 1944 he was appointed Port Warden in Montreal and served in that capacity until 1950. However, like many of the survivors, his health had been affected by the gassing and he returned to England where he worked as a North Sea Pilot.

He died on 31st August 1952 aged 55 years, whilst boarding an American T.2. tanker and buried in his native Chester- Le -Street.

EMPIRE SAILOR. [Alan Fairley]

EMPIRE SAILOR as CELLINA under Italian ownership in 1935 [N.M.M.]

(7e). **Ernest CAIRNS** - Master Mariner.

"What's that astern of us daddy!"

Ernest Cairns joined the Merchant Navy on 27th December, 1916, at the age of 16 years. He signed an ordinary apprentice's indenture, being allowed £40 as follows:

£5   1st. year
£8   2nd year
£12   3rd year
£15   4th and final year

With an allowance of 12 shillings (60p) per annum for washing and a gratuity of £5, should he complete the indenture satisfactorily.

Document:
NAVAL SERVICE HISTORY OF LT.ERNEST CAIRNS 10.2.1941.
On 31st July 1920 until 9th May 1923, Ernest sailed as an A.B. with Sutherland S.S. Co. Ltd. on the KINCARDINE (2) and with Denholm Line Steamers Ltd. of Glasgow, onboard MYRTLE PARK.

On 2nd July 1923, he sailed as 2nd Mate on HEATH PARK (2), CARRONPARK and BROOMPARK (3) until June 1926. He then sailed as 2nd Mate onboard KINROSS (IV) for The Shipping Controller, under management of the Sutherland S.S. Co. Ltd, and later still as 2nd Mate on the HOLMPARK (2) of Denholm's.

Ernest gained his Masters certificate on 19th December, 1928 and on the 4th March 1929, Ernest sailed as 3rd Mate on the M.V. CLAM (2) tanker, for Shell U.K. Then from 1st January,1930 until 30th January, 1940, Ernest sailed with The Cairn Line of Steamships, as follows:

CAIRNROSS (III)	3rd MATE	5- VOYAGES
CAIRMONA (I)	2nd MATE	2- VOYAGES
CAIRNVALONA	2nd MATE	13-VOYAGES
	1st MATE	21-VOYAGES

From 14th March, 1940 until 4th November, 1940, Ernest sailed as 3rd Mate with Manchester Liners Ltd. onboard MANCHESTER EXPORTER(I) being promoted to 2nd Mate on 18th October, 1940.

During W.W.II. Ernest was commissioned Lieutenant R.N.R. His daughters, Margaret Shipley and Dorothy Baxter said he was invalided out, being quite ill, weighing just six and a half stone.

However, in 1947 Ernest returned to sea sailing for The Ministry of War Transport-under management of the Sutherland S.S. Co. Ltd. onboard the FORT SOURIS, North Sands Type freighter for 4 voyages, as 2nd Mate then 1st Mate. From 24th January, 1948 until 30th April, 1949, he joined the M.V. CROMARTY(IV) of The Sutherland S.S. Co. Ltd. under charter to the Palm Line of London.

Ernest joined Thos. & Jas. Harrison's Chartente Steamship Co. Ltd of Liverpool and from 25th May, 1949 until 27th October, 1955 he sailed on their ships, mostly home trade and coasting- seven times as 3rd Mate and thirty eight times 2nd Mate:

PHILOSPHER, SENATOR, HISTORIAN, GEOLOGIST, ADVISOR, MV STATESMEN, DALESMAN, PROSPECTOR, TRADER, SETTLER, SCHOLAR, STRATEGIST, INVENTOR, NATURALIST, NOVELIST, MV HERDSMAN, SELECTOR, CRAFTSMAN, EXPLORER, SPECIALIST, WANDERER, ARBRITRATOR, CROFTER, BIOGRAPHER, STUDENT.

Ernest then rejoined the Cairn Line of Steamships, sailing as 2nd Mate on the CAIRNGOWAN(IV) under (Captain I G Foster) then from 9th January, 1956 until 15th July1957 sailed on the CAIRNAVON(IV), as 1st Mate for 7 voyages (two with Captain J. Hogg). His daughters, Margaret and Dorothy believe Ernest sailed on the CAIRNFORTH sometime from 1958 onwards. However his 3rd discharge book has been misplaced. The book goes up to 1965, when Ernest decided to call it a day.

WAR MEDALS AND COMMENDATIONS
ERNEST CAIRNS
MASTER MARINER
1939 TO 1945 WAR MEDAL
1939 TO 1945 STAR
1941 TO 1945 BURMA STAR

S.S. CAIRNVALONA – Ernest as 1st Mate.

96

(7f.) **William Stanley WILKINSON.**   Chief Engineer.

In 1894, William Stanley Wilkinson was born, and at the age of 12, became a riveters boy' with George T. Grey, Engine Builders and Repairers, of South Shields. In July 1916, he joined the Watts Watts Company's BLACKHEATH as 4th Engineer for two trips.

Stan and' Mate'

In April 1919, Stan joined the CAIRNGOWAN(III) as 3rd Engineer and served on the following Cairn Line ships:

CAIRNDHU(III)	2nd Engineer.	1922.
CAIRNROSS(III)	3rd then 2nd Engineer	1926.
CAIRNGLEN(II)	2nd Engineer.	1934.
CAIRNESK(III)	Chief Engineer.	1938.
CAIRNGOWAN(IV)	Chief Engineer.	1952.

On 24th November, 1959, he retired.

[*Note:* On the 10th January, 1945, West of Gibraltar, the BLACKHEATH, 4,637grt. (Watts, Watts Co. Ltd) on a voyage from U.K. for Italy was torpedoed and sunk by UB.870.]
Stanley Jnr. has stated that during W.W.II. the CAIRNESK (III) was used several times as the Commodore ship in convoys.
Besides being an excellent ship for sailing the North Atlantic Ocean, the CAIRNESK (III) was fitted with the following armaments:
At stern: - 3.7 gun and 2 depth charges
On bridge: - 2 X 20mm oerlekins and 2 Hotchkiss heavy machine guns, also a
                   wire parachute rocket, for low flying aircraft!!!.

CAIRNROSS (III)

WAR MEDALS AND COMMENDATIONS
WILLIAM STANLEY WILKINSON
CHIEF ENGINEER
1914 - 1918 WAR MEDAL
1914 - 1918 MERCANTILE MARINE MEDAL
1939 - 1945 WAR MEDAL
1939 - 1945 ATLANTIC STAR
1939 - 1945 STAR

(7g.) Ian GRANT FOSTER – Master Mariner.

The following is a letter from Marion Foster, daughter of Captain Ian Grant Foster:

Northumberland

2nd. November, 2006.

My father left Woodside Secondary School in Glasgow in October, 1918. Between 1918 and 1922 my dad served as an apprentice with the Glasgow shipping company, H. Hogarth & Sons. His first ship was the WAR DUCK but most of his four years was spent on the S.S. BARON BLANTYRE.

He then joined the City Line and was 4th Officer on the troop ship CITY OF MARSEILLES, trooping between Southampton and India. The vessel was laid up in March 1924 when trooping ended, so my father signed on with the CITY OF VENICE until he was promoted to 3rd Officer with the S.S .CITY OF ORAN in September 1924. These voyages took him from the U.S.A . to the Far East, India, China, Japan. He remained with the City Line for some years on the CITY OF CALCUTTA, CITY OF MANCHESTER and CITY OF CAMBRIDGE, holding the rank of 2nd Officer, travelling to South Africa and Australia.

In 1933, the continued depression in shipping hit companies hard and my father was one of the many sailors laid off. However, my father found a post on another ship within a month, sailing with the M.V. BRITISH SCIENCE for the next year (The B.T.C Company). He went on to sail with the S.S .HARMANTEH (J. & C. Harrison Ltd)of London. 1935-1938 and then S.S. HARBLEDOWN with the same company.

In March 1939 he became 1st Officer on the S.S. MAINDY HILL which was sunk a year later on 9th March 1940 in the North Sea. I don't know if any men were lost, but I know my father lost all his possessions and turned up at home in borrowed clothes, much to my mothers shock-and relief. I know the Master, Captain D. A. Johnson survived because I still have a letter from him to my father, sent from his Edinburgh home a few days later.

Within weeks my father became Chief Officer of the S.S. WHITE CREST with Hall Bros. of Newcastle, for 3 months. Then the S.S. CADUCEUS, and on 3rd June, 1942 he joined the S.S. EMPIRE SNOW as Chief Officer. At the time the vessel belonged to Joseph Constantine Steamships but in December that year it was transferred to the Cairn Line and my father transferred with it .

It was during this period when my father was mentioned in despatches, twice, first in June 1941 for action, while aboard the S.S .WHITE CREST in the Summer of 1940:

The ship had encountered enemy submarines, aircraft and ships, If I remember correctly, from a childhood memory, of a funny story my father used to tell. The ship was torpedoed but the bomb didn't explode. Somehow they had to disarm it and seal the hole in the hull. My father used to make us laugh as he described hanging over the side , half in the water, helping to patch up the damage. He said the ships cat licked the torpedo and was blowing green bubbles afterwards! He spoke very little of the war years and always made light of his experiences.

11. October '42

IMPIRE SNOW.
Archangel.
11th Oct '42.

Received from above Steamer.
53 (fifty three) bales
Polish Comforts. and
64 (Sixty four) Cases
perspex glass,

СОЛОБАЛА   АРХАНГЕЛЬСК

and to this day no one knows what the "53 BALES OF "POLISH COMFORTS" were. The only sensible suggestion was made in recent years by Captain Alan Fairley, twice, he went to Russia with the North Sea Convoys, and said the women sailors in Russia were as big as men-and thereby lies a mystery. He got one of them to sign a receipt for some later cargo (who had been an officer under my father's command many years). He believes they were bales of clothing and blankets for Polish.

Father retired from sea in the 1960's. He took up a Superintendents post after a heart attack forced him to 'swallow the anchor and come Refugees, who were living in refugee camps, having fled to Russia from the Nazis in Poland, however, I have not been able to confirm if this suggestion is correct.

My father was commended again in 1943 for his experiences on the S.S EMPIRE SNOW on those convoys to Russia.

After he died I was looking through his papers and wallet and found two sheets of folded paper tucked away in a forgotten corner they were rather fragile and slightly damaged by an ink spill. I opened them up carefully and discovered a detailed description of two days in September 1942 when the EMPIRE SNOW was the "leading ship 3rd line port" and facing enemy action. The description is calm and unemotional but reading it always makes my heart beat faster as I feel the tension in his words.

My father spent the war on North Atlantic, Russian and Mediterranean convoys and somehow got through it all. I was born in the middle of it all in March 1943 and of course remember nothing of those anxious days.

By the time I am old enough to remember life on board ships, the war was over, and my father was Captain on the CAIRNESK (III).

My parents did tell me I learned to stand up on my own for the first time while onboard the EMPIRE SNOW. They would sit me on a couch below a port hole in my father's cabin and tie my safety reins to the big brass handle on the port hole. I gather the sight of me pulling my weight against the reins and heaving myself upright caused me and my parents huge delight and a lot of laughter. Later my two younger brothers were to get their sea legs on board the CAIRNESK (III). In 1952 my father took command of the new S.S. CAIRNGOWAN (IV), which remained a home from home for us until we grew up.

My father always like to make us laugh and was full of fun. The ships crew were his family so they were our family too. We were brought up to respect and be respectful to everyone on board.

Marion Foster.

> **WAR MEDALS AND COMMENDATIONS**
> **IAN GRANT FOSTER**
> **MASTER MARINER**
>
> 1939 - 1945 STAR
> 1939 - 1945 ATLANTIC STAR
> 1939 - 1945 WAR MEDAL
> 1939 - 1945 ARTIC EMBLEM
> COMMENDATION FOR BRAVERY
> MENTIONED IN DISPATCHES

CAIRNGOWAN(IV) in ice, St. Lawrence River : 1955   [MARION FOSTER]

The following documents are listed as follows:

1   MENTIONED IN DISPATCHES 1941 AND 1943

By the KING'S Order the name of
Ian Grant Foster,
First Mate, s.s. "Whitecrest,"
was published in the London Gazette on
10 June, 1941,
as commended for brave conduct in the
Merchant Navy.
I am charged to record His Majesty's
high appreciation of the service rendered.

[signature]

Prime Minister and First Lord
of the Treasury

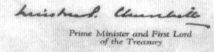

MERCHANT NAVY HONOURS.

Six Service Awards for Russian Passage.

An Admiralty list of awards, published in
last night's "London Gazette", included the
following decorations for officers and men of the
Merchant Navy:-

For coolness, courage and devotion to duty
under relentless attacks by the enemy while on
passage to North Russia:-

The Distinguished Service Cross.

Captain Murdo Macleod, Master.
Mr. James William Trueman, Chief Engineer Officer.

The Distinguished Service Medal.

Chief Steward William Hamilton.
Boatswain James Moar, B.E.M.

Mention in Despatches.

Mr. Ian Grant Foster, Chief Officer.
Mr. Geoffrey Chester, Second Officer.

(7h.) **Albert James DUNN**. – Master Mariner.

Albert was born 7th June 1899 at Staithes, NorthYorkshire. He became an apprentice with the Whitby shipowners, Rowland & Marwood, serving on steamer RYDE between October 1918 until March 1921. On the latter date, Albert joined the Ice breaker ANNAPOLIS.(889grt./.1898)O.N.10669. in Canada Between 30th July 1924 and 9th January. 1930, Albert sailed as 3rd Mate/2nd Mate, on the CAIRNDHU(III), CAIRNVALONA and CAIRNROSS(III). On7thApril,1933, he became 1st Mate on CAIRNROSS(III) and later Albert was appointed Master, serving on the EMPIRE LAPWING, CAIRNESK (III), EMPIRE SAILOR, and CAIRNVALONA, until 21st October 1944. Unfortunately, Albert had to retire due to ill health.

During his service Albert was awarded:

WAR MEDALS
ALBERT JAMES DUNN
MASTER MARINER
1939 TO 1945 STAR
1939 TO 1945 ATLANTIC STAR
1939 TO 1945 WAR MEDAL

Note: Captain Dunn's daughters, Irene and Dorothy (both living in New South Wales, Australia) told the author that their father was injured when the CAIRNROSS (III) was mined and sunk in the River Mersey on 6 January 1940. They thought the Master was named Halcrow.
The following photos were gifted by Captain Dunn's daughters:
1.   CAIRNROSS (III) Passing under the JACQUES CARTIER Bridge.
2.   Dad – on CAIRNROSS(III).
3.   Dad – standing on the Left and Stan WILKINSON and Captain HALCROW seated.
4.   Dad – Third from the right and Stan WILKINSON second from the right.
These photos were all taken pre -war and I would think on the CAIRNROSS (III). Sadly we don't have any shipboard photos of dad after he became Captain on a photo taken by a friend at their home in Montreal. Dad was superstitious of having photos taken in wartime!!

CAIRNROSS(III) passing under the Jacques Cartier Bridge.

DAD onboard CAIRNROSS(III).

Dad standing far left of Stan Wilkinson and Captain Halcrow.(Both seated.)
with John Smith (Third Officer) extreme right.

Dad (third Right) with Stan Wilkinson to his left and Captain MELLING (Fourth from right.)

CAIRNROSS (III) (1921-1940)

O.N. 145449   5494 g 3262 n   425 x 55 x 26.6 feet

3 x Parson Marine Turbines, double reduction geared to a single screw shaft, by Parsons Marine Turbine Co. Ltd., Newcastle

25/11/1920 Launched by The Sunderland Shipbuilding Co. Ltd., Sunderland (Yard No. 322) for the Cairn Line of Steamships Ltd. (Cairns Noble & Co. Ltd., managers).

6/1/1940 Sunk by mine laid by U30 off River Mersey in Convoy OB74 on voyage from Tyne, Leith & Liverpool to St. Johns (NB) with coal & general cargo. Crew all saved.

CAIRNROSS (III) – *National Maritime Museum Greenwich*

CAIRNVALONA (1918-

O.N. 140718   6402 g 4566 n   415.2 x 53.1 x 25.2 feet

T. 3 cylinder (28", 46" & 75" x 51") engine by Blair & Co., Stockton-on- Tees. 550 nhp.

10/4/1918 Launched by Sunderland Shipbuilding Co. Ltd., Sunderland (Yard No. 314) for the Cairn Line of Steamships Ltd (Cairns Noble & Co., managers) Newcastle.

8/5/1918 Under tow from River Wear to Teesside for engine installation, a torpedo was fired at her, which missed. Vessel was able to continue on into the Tees where the engines were subsequently fitted by Blair & Co. at Stockton.

8/1918 Completed.

24/10/1940 On voyage from Montreal to Tyne, with general cargo, was attacked by aircraft, but escaped serious damage and arrived Leith on 28/10/1940.

9/4/43 Whilst in Convoy ON176, was accidentally in collision with the Norwegian manned destroyer HMS BEVERLEY (Ex USS BRANCH/1920), which sustained severe damage including the loss of her Asdic capability. The warship was unable to keep up with the convoy, and on 11/4/1943 was torpedoed and sunk by U188, with the loss of all but 4 of the ship's company of 152, some of whom were accidentally depth charged by another destroyer escort attending the sinking.

1952 Sold to BISCO for scrap.

30/6/1952 Arrived at Clayton & Davies breaking yard, Dunston-on-Tyne.

CAIRNVALONA – *National Maritime Museum Greenwich*

(7i). Andrew GUILD – Boatswain. B.E.M.

Andrew was born on 1st May. 1895, at Newhaven, Edinburgh. He joined the Merchant Navy in August, 1919, as an A.B. onboard CAIRNGOWAN(III). Andrew stayed with this ship until 17th January 1938. Later on 19th February 1940 he was appointed Bosun on the CAIRNGLEN(II). On 10th January 1941, he joined the DAGOMBA still as Bosun. In May, 1941, Andrew joined, as Bosun, the CAIRNESK(III), remaining as such till 5th December 1951.

Unfortunately Andrew was killed in a railway accident. He was sadly missed by all who knew him.

WAR MEDALS
ANDREW GUILD B.E.M.(CIVIL)
BOATSWAIN

1939 TO 1945 STAR
1939 TO 1945 ATLANTIC STAR
1939 TO 1945 WAR MEDAL

(7j.) **Sydney Whayman PARKS,** - Master Mariner.

THE PARKS FAMILY.

Sydney Parks joined in 1914, serving 4 years as a Cadet with Watts & Watts Co. In 1923 Sydney joined the Cairn Line, serving onboard - SCATWELL, CAIRNMONA(II), CAIRNGOWAN (III), CAIRNVALONA, and the EMPIRE BRIGADE. On 18 October 1940 the EMPIRE BRIGADE in convoy SC7 was torpedoed and sank. Captain Sydney Parks and 34 crew were rescued by H.MS.FOWEY, a sloop built 1930, 1,105grt and landed at Greenock (Lt. Commander C. G. De Bush).

His son F. H. Parkes, Master Mariner stated that in late 1940, the Cairn Line was to receive two Black Diamond ships, and Captain Parks took command of the BLACK OSPREY. .

BLACK OSPREY   WORLD SHIP SOCIETY

On 18 September 1941, the BLACK OSPREY was torpedoed by U96, south of Iceland. Captain Parks and 24 crew were lost.

(7k). **Joseph BELL** – Boatswain.

Joe joined the Merchant Navy in 1936, sailing out of Newcastle-Upon-Tyne. In 19 years service he sailed on 75 trips, of which 41 were with the Cairn Line.

His ships included WENTWORTH, BRITISH UNION, BACKWORTH (this ship managed to sail through the Spanish blockade of Bilboa Docks, during the Spanish Civil War) and HOOKWOOD. In 1939 the HOOKWOOD struck a magnetic mine, off Tonque light vessel, with loss of two crew. Joe couldn't swim, but grabbed some timber, in the freezing sea, thinking it was 'his last' but survived. (see report-Gazette 18 November, 1999).

His next ship was the South Metropolitan Gas Company collier CATFORD, but had to abandon the ship again on 31/5/1943 after striking a mine in the North Sea. 4 crew and 5 DEMS gunners were lost. The survivors only spent an hour in the lifeboats, before being rescued by the Thames tug SUN. IV. Joe had earlier served the on BIDDLESTONE, then EMPIRE BOND, EMPIRE MOORHEN and BARRWHIN.

Between 1942/43 he served on EMPIRE DACE (naval ferry), sailing between Gibraltar and African Coast, carrying troops and tanks to the beaches. (On 1 December 1944, whilst in the entrance of Missolonghi Harbour, the EMPIRE DACE was sunk by a mine).

Joe had previously left and served on EMPIRE FOAM, CHIGNECTO PARK and EMPIRE SNOW, later renamed CAIRNAVON (IV). Afterwards he was on FULHAM (II), COULMORE before joining the CAIRNESK (III) on 10th December 1946.

Joe then sailed on various other ships, namely, HOPERANGE, SOUTHWOOD, CROMARTY and SPERO. On 14th December 1949, the SPERO's engine room flooded, taking a severe list to port. The crew abandoned ship and were picked up by a fishery rescue vessel and landed at Esjberg, Denmark. Later came the HIGHLAND, BRITISH COUNCILLOR, WILLIAM PEARMAN and then CAIRNVALONA (Bosun).

On 14th July 1952, Joe signed as Bosun, on the CAIRNGOWAN (IV) (Master, Captain Ian Grant Foster), for 23 trips until 15th September 1955, when he 'swallowed the anchor'.
I am sure readers will agree that Joe had his share of luck.

WAR MEDALS AND COMMENDATIONS
JOSEPH BELL
BOATSWAIN

1939 - 1945 STAR
1939 - 1945 ATLANTIC STAR
1939 - 1945 WAR MEDAL
1940 - 1943 AFRICA STAR & CLASP

MY AMAZING ESCAPE

Pensioner recounts part in wartime shipwreck drama

By TERRY KELLY

LOOKING BACK ... former able seaman Joe Bell. (C14358)

THEN ... Joe relives his tale 60 years ago, left, and his log book, right.

A PENSIONER told today how he amazingly survived a wartime shipwreck drama - exactly 60 years ago.

Former Merchant Navy able seaman Joe Bell, 79, of York Street, Jarrow, clung onto a piece of wood in the freezing-cold North Sea for several hours after his ship was blown up by a magnetic mine in November, 1939.

Joe was a non-swimmer and admits he thought he would die after his ship, the Hookwood, sank in a matter of minutes.

He said: "We heard this terrific sound and the ship seemed to just break in half.

"The decks were afloat straight away and I found myself in the water, clinging onto a 15ft long piece of wood.

"I thought my end had come. I've never learnt to swim and I thought there was no way we were going to survive. The water was freezing and my fellow crewmen were all around me."

Nineteen-year-old Merchant seaman Joe had only joined the Hookwood out of Blyth Harbour a few days before disaster struck.

Another Jarrow crewman on the ship was George Craig, nicknamed "Crasher," who waited in the cold North Sea with Joe to be rescued.

Thankfully, after more than two hours, the two South Tyneside men were picked up by an Allied vessel, but two Scottish sailors died when the ship sank.

The two borough sailors and their fellow crewmen were taken to a hospital in Chatham to recover.

HOOKWOOD 1939

(7L). **Needham Edwin FORTH** - Master Mariner.

"From the age of five I was obsessed with ships and the sea. I used to drag my poor Mother around the various ferries and docks on the Tyne. Though my Father had been killed at sea in 1930 it didn't deter me. I had failed the 11 plus exam, so to boost my chances of getting to sea went to the Marine School of South Shields for what was called a pre-apprenticeship course. After three months at this I joined Stott, Mann & Fleming's M.V. HOPEPEAK as Cadet in March 1938. This ship was still building at Swan Hunters when I was appointed, so I was able to see here and see what I was getting into. The M.V. HOPEPEACK was a Doxford engined 12 knots tramp steamer built 'on spec' by Swan's, then hired out to Stott, Mann and Fleming. We sailed on 'April fools day' 1938, being cheered all the way down the river. What a difference to today's empty uncaring river. I watched the Tyne pilot leaving us and even then at 16, I thought, that's the job for me one day.

My first voyage was ideal in that we went round the world in six months. My fellow cadets and I both 'widows mites', were amazed at the new swear words we learnt and the hard graft we were subject to-we got all the dirty work-cleaning bilges, tanks etc. We hadn't been at sea a week before one of the ordinary seamen fell from the shifting boards to the bottom of the hold and was killed. His effects were sold by auction and I remember it raised 7/6d. The ship owner graciously added £5 to this! I also had to face the fact that I suffered from sea sickness. This plagued me for the rest of my career. After six months we returned to Liverpool.

As Cadets we were free to leave HOPEPEAK when we got to the UK–which we did – infuriating the owners who switched to 'Apprentice's, bound for four years thereafter. For some crazy reason my fellow cadet and I both fancied going into 'Tankers'. Anyway we both went back to the Marine School. I ended up with C.T. Bowring Tankers while he went to Anglo-Saxon and eventually became Marine Supt. there, I was going to be Bowring's first apprentice for many years and was appointed to their M.V. EL MIRLO on 3rd January 1939. The wisdom of going into tankers with the war clouds looming points to the 'recklessness of youth'.

EL MIRLO carried highly dangerous benzine from Peru to Manchester every 2 months. War broke out in September 1939 and we were fitted with a 1917, 4.7 Japanese gun, give a little training in Cammell Lairds and told to 'get on with it'. A gun platform had already been fitted a year before. We were all petrified when we had to have a practice shoot. I was sight-setter at side of the gun and the 2nd Mate was trembling as he pulled the trigger! The blast was fantastic but we all survived. Fortunately we never had to fire it again in anger.

I had a comfortable 19 months on EL MIRLO as it was such a success! They sent me another apprentice, after sailing alone for six months. What a life for two young men though. We worked 4 on 4 off at sea and 6 on 6 off in port on cargo duties – even in the UK. The only time I got home was when we had a minor collision in the Mersey and had to dry dock. Enemy action-wise we were lucky in EL MIRLO. In convoy most of the time we saw very little of the enemy. Lots of depth charging but few sinkings. We actually lost our convoy once and made it all the way on our own.

At the ripe old age of 19, I felt it was about time to help my Mother financially. Explaining this to Bowring's they very decently allowed me to cancel my indentures allowing me to go to sea as an Ordinary Seaman where I would earn the princely sum of £17 per month, including war bonus. £10 which I sent to my mother. As an apprentice I was getting £2 per month, but after I left Bowring's, apprentices were also given the war bonus, so I wasn't that much better off. With hindsight I should have stayed an apprentice, for I now spent three very uncomfortable voyages as a 'Sailor'–a war time rating in between O.S. and A.B. The first the BRITISH DESTINY, a miserable 5 month voyage to the Persian Gulf via the Cape of Good Hope. Next a horrible open bridge (no wheel house) ship called TREHATA to Canada. Finally, and worst of all the BARON KINNAIRD to Georgetown, B.G.(British Guiana) to load bauxite. We lived forward in this ship and were thrown about all over the place–getting food up forward when shipping heavy seas was a problem. Eventually we ran out of food and survived on lifeboat rations before arriving at our first port – Port Arthur, Texas. The only good thing that came out of my forecastle experience was that it made me determined to get out of it. So while my fellow sailors played cards at one end of the table I studied hard for my 2nd Mates certificate, not an easy thing to do.

After 3 months at 'Nellists' Nautical School, I got my 2nd Mates certificate. In those days you got no money while studying ashore, so you couldn't afford to hang about. I signed on with the Shipping Federation, Newcastle and was immediately sent to join the S.S. HARTLEBURY, loading 'munitions' at Sunderland for Russia! This was on the 4th May 1942, we proceeded to Iceland, where we lay for a month while the ill fated convoy P.Q.17 was assembled with a huge Naval backup. I wont dwell on the much documented voyage, which resulted in the convoy being scattered and 28 ships being sunk. All the ships were well armed and we had beaten off several air attacks. The 2nd Mate and I manned a machine gun on the bridge and enjoyed blazing away at the Junkers 88's as they came in at mast height, helping to shoot down the leading plane. Flushed with success we were dismayed when the convoy was told to scatter and our naval escort fled. We knew it was only a matter of time and spent the next 24 hours listening to the numerous S.O.S. messages as the U-boats picked off the unprotected ships.

Our turn came on the 7th July 1942. I was on watch at the time and the first torpedo struck just below me on the starboard wing of the bridge. The blast of the explosion actually threw me through the air across the wheelhouse. We had Oerlikon gun nests on platforms each side of the wheelhouse, manned by Maritime Army Gunners. These came crashing down and I never saw the soldiers again. Captain Stevenson, a tough little Yorkshire man, was also stuck by the falling Oerlikon platform and sustained injuries from which he died many months later. A second torpedo stuck just below the starboard lifeboat, putting that out of action. Before I got down to my lifeboat on the port side, a crowd of stewards and firemen had jumped aboard causing the apprentice to let go the after falls, tipping the boat stern first into the sea and the occupants with it. The same thing happened with the jolly boat, which somehow was capsized, depositing more people into the water. The 1st Mate had managed to launch a large raft from the shrouds of the foremast. He cast off and managed to pick up about ten men from the water. That left my lifeboat hanging from the forward falls with the stern full of water. I slid down the falls and joined about a dozen other crew in the waterlogged boat. Somebody cast off the painter without orders leaving the poor 2nd Mate stranded aboard. The ship still had headway so when the painter was released we drifted rapidly down the portside. At this point we were struck by a third torpedo and the ship keeled over us and we though she was going to capsize and take us with her. However, we drifted clear. The third torpedo had broken the ships back and she sank with bow and stern in the air. At the last moment the Captain jumped from the stern and we were able to pull him aboard. The HARTLEBURY sank in seven minutes. In that time we had been torn from our warm, comfortable, well fed life to sitting in a waterlogged lifeboat, up to our waist in water temp. 36 ° F (it was summer or it could have been worse). Fortunately the sea was calm, but with just enough swell to keep our lifeboat full, kept afloat by buoyancy tanks. The German Sub surfaced and came within hailing distance asking for the Captain. Fortunately the Captain was not in uniform and we pretended he'd gone down with the ship. Their Captain then asked a very interesting question – why are you fighting for the Communists? – none of us could answer that one. They then passed us a bottle of Schnapps and some black bread and told us land was only 7 miles away, ignoring the fact that we were just about under water. There was twenty of us aboard. Those fortunate enough to be huddled in the bow and stern were out of the water, but the rest of us were sitting waist deep in water and hypothermia quickly began to take its toll. Within an hour we lost one fireman quickly, followed by the wireless operator and the elderly Chief Engineer. All these poor chaps had no protective clothing and soon succumbed. I had my special Arctic gear on but my shoes had dropped off, so I took the poor dead wireless operators sea-boots off and put them on. The symptoms of hypothermia seemed to be drowsiness, then falling asleep, then death. There were only two of us left in the water – we tried to get an oar out but couldn't turn the boat head into the waves at all. I was beginning to feel drowsy myself now and made the decision that saved my life. I forced my way up on to the stern sheets of the lifeboat. The lifeboat was so low in the water that bailing her out was impossible so we had to take the decision to get rid of the dead. There were five of us left now, Captain, myself, 2nd Mate Steward, O.S. and a fireman. Without ceremony we pushed our shipmates over the side-fifteen in all. We then quickly bailed the boat out and with a struggle managed to get the mast up. Having helped us and worked hard, we were amazed when the firemen – a young Latvian, seemed to go off his head and jumped overboard and swam away from us vanishing into the mist. We were now able to get the lifeboats sail up and actually began to make headway drifting away from the bodies of the dead crew members. We had been shrouded in mist since being torpedoed – I think if we had been able to see the coast of the island of Novaya Zembla only 7 miles away, our unfortunate ship-mates might have survived longer than they did. By a remarkable stroke of luck out of the mist came the 1st Mates raft with ten crew on board. While so many of the lifeboats crew had died, those on the raft seemed fit and well. The raft was a simple structure built around four or six oil drums, but it had a freeboard of about two feet, keeping those who could hang on to it dry and this is what saved them. Anyway they leapt aboard the lifeboat and soon had her bailed out and the sail properly set. They transferred the rafts provisions and we now had our first meal of pemmican and chocolate. Confident now that we had survived and would soon be rescued, we bumped ashore on Goose Island, a small uninhabited Island off Novaya Zembla in Lat 74° N long 55° E.

The sun never sets in these 'lats' and so we had little idea of the time. We pulled the boat ashore and set up camp under the lifeboat sail, got a fire going and looked around the island. We found nothing but numerous goose eggs, which we quickly cooked and ate – very nice, though rather fishy. After a nights rest we awoke next day to find a ship several miles away but obviously aground. We immediately got under way again and headed towards her. We had lost all of our oars so had to rely on sails. As we got closed to the ship, we were amazed when she lowered her lifeboats and came to our rescue. The ship turned out to be the American WINSTON SALEM one of the convoy. Rather than suffer the same fate as the rest of us the Captain had deliberately run her ashore. She was eventually towed off and made it back to the for repairs, one of the few ships of P.Q.17 that did so. We were fed like 'fighting cocks' and they gave us clothing, seemingly off their own backs. We feared air attacks now, of course, but a Russian plane saw us first and a small Russian vessel – which I have completely forgotten – arrived and transferred us all to the M.V. EMPIRE TIDE one of the convoy which was sheltering at anchor further down the coast. This was a 'CAM' ship I.e. she was armed with a Hurricane plane and a catapult. This seemed to keep the German planes away even though it was never used. There must have been a couple of hundred survivors aboard the EMPIRE TIDE and the Chief Steward did a marvellous job feeding us all. Our Captain was in a bad way and he was flown home from here, but sadly died of his wounds later. The rest of us were landed aboard the corvette LA MALOUINE and transferred to Archangel. We landed in Archangel on 25th July 1942, with nothing but the clothes on our backs. I had frost-bitten toes and my fellow survivor from the lifeboat Asst. Steward Spayler a badly frost-bitten foot, which later had to be amputated. We spent the rest of the summer in the Intoursit Hotel. Rowing, playing chess, waiting for ever for our meals to be served and secretly dreading our return voyage to the U.K.

Eventually we were loaded aboard the rescue ship ZAMALEK and sailed in convoy Q.P.14 on 13th September. Things were quiet until 20th September when we were soon in action picking up survivors from the four ships and three escort vessels which were lost in this convoy. The Commodore of the convoy, an elderly R.N. Officer who had lost his ship in P.Q.17 was again torpedoed in OCEAN VOICE in this convoy. We had air cover in this convoy for the first time provided by the small carrier AVENGER whose swordfish planes managed to sink a couple of U-boats although the weather was too bad for launching planes most of the time. We reached Loch Ewe on 26th September, after a fortnight at sea, living in bunks in the 'tween decks, waiting for a torpedo to come through the hull. From Loch Ewe we were transferred to the Irish Ferry MUNSTER. We arrived in Glasgow on 28th September 1942 but instead of being allowed home we survivors (1,500 in all) were taken to St Andrews Hall for a civic reception and a 'pep' talk by the M.O.W.T. Mr Noel Baker saying whatever the cost it had been worth it. This speech was howled down by everyone present. We were given a 'survivors suit and sent on our way.

I was back at sea on the 24th October 1942, this time as 3rd Mae on the EMPIRE CAXTON. This ship was only 3,000grt. built for the Baltic timber trade rather than the North Atlantic, but such was the state of British Merchant Shipping that with the best of our ships being sunk by U-boats, we were really 'scraping the barrel'. I always believed that the American 'Liberty ship' won the war for us. It was only when they began arriving in huge numbers that the war turned in our favour. I had an uncomfortable voyage in EMPIRE CAXTON loading bauxite in Georgetown, British Guiana. On the return Atlantic crossing we were attacked by U-boats in the middle of the night in atrocious weather. I think we lost about ten ships. One ship was torpedoed but stayed afloat while the unfortunate crew took to the lifeboats and were never seen again! Meanwhile, our little ship became a straggler – unable to keep up with the rest of the convoy. So we had a few anxious hours until the weather moderated and we caught the convoy up. I was glad to sign-off this ship in Cardiff on the 20th March, 1943. I thought the best way of survival in the war was to change ships every voyage and let fate take care of me. Two of my old ships had been sunk after I left them so maybe I was right.

My next ship was the CLAN MURRAY joining her in Glasgow on 10th April 1943. She was loading 'munitions' for the North Africa campaign. The cargo was being loaded by the Army working round the clock, the Glasgow dockers being on strike! Shortly afterwards Glasgow was 'blitzed' by the Luftwaffe. Next day the dockers returned to work. We sailed in convoy backing up the landing in North Africa. Under air and sea attack all the way we discharged our cargo at Bone in North Africa, about as far east as the Allies had got. We were under constant air attack while discharging, enjoying the terrific anti-aircraft barrage put up the H.M.S DIDO with all ten of her 5.25" guns blazing away. The Arab dockers took to the hills as soon as the air raid sirens began, so discharging was a slow business. From Bone we sailed in ballast to West Africa where we loaded with palm kernels. Once loaded we sailed for Liverpool arriving in late August 1943. Liverpool had been blitzed when we got there and the Mersey was littered with sunken ships. I had only been 4th Mate on the CLAN MURRAY so I left the Clan Line looking for more responsibility. Someone had told me that we could transfer from Newcastle 'Pool' or Shipping Federation to the Liverpool 'Pool'.

After a spell at home I did this and was immediately appointed 2nd Mate of the S.S. FORT ESPERANCE. This ship was still building in Canada and to get there we sailed in the MAURITANIA now acting as a troopship. Quite enjoyed being a passenger for the first time in my life. We had an uneventful crossing, sailing without escort to New York and thence by train to Montreal. Our new ship – the Canadian version of the Liberty Ship – I believe both types have the same hull shape – awaited us. We loaded 'munitions' for London Docks, arriving just before Christmas 1943. The passage had been uneventful apart from the usual depth charging going on. I 'paid off' the FORT ESPERANCE in London and after a fortnights leave I foolishly signed on the Newcastle 'Pool' again and was sent to join the S.S. FRAMLINGTON COURT. The last time I saw this old ship she had been mined and run ashore on the beach at South Shields. She had been patched up on the Tyne and off we sailed, via Hull, to the West Coast of Africa. The voyage was uneventful and I can't remember what cargo we brought home. Paid off in Liverpool on 24th April 1944, after 3 months.

Once again I decided to transfer to the 'Liverpool Pool', for my next ship, and once again I found myself a passenger on the MAURITANIA, this time to join a new building Liberty Ship the SAMTANA at Baltimore.

I was in a hotel and I switched on the bedside radio to hear that the 'D Day' landings had commenced. I was young enough to feel sorry that I had missed it all. The war was switching to Japan now and we were soon on our way loaded with 'munitions,' vehicles etc bound for Bombay. Our first stop on the long voyage East was Bari in Italy, the Germans having retreated from the Mediterranean by now. Their bombers were still at work however and Bari had been heavily blitzed just before we got there. An amazing sight was the entire superstructure of an American Liberty Ship blown ¾ mile inland from the harbour. We proceeded through Suez and on to various Indian ports finishing up in Calcutta. Switching from the threat of U-boats to the threat of Japanese subs in the Indian Ocean. Sailed from Calcutta on 12th October 1944 and arrived in Newcastle on 10th December 1944. I can remember nothing of this long voyage until we got into home waters. In an east coast convoy bound for the Tyne the whole starboard column of the convoy ran aground. We blamed the Naval escort for this of course. We were third ship of four and as we struck I went on the starboard side of the lower bridge to be presented with a ship bow bearing down on us – this was the fourth ship of the convoy. I beat a hasty retreat as she stuck us just under the bridge. She did us quite a bit of damage to the hull, fortunately all above the waterline. This was the only collision in the convoy and we were all able to resume as the tide rose. We eventually arrived at the River Tyne – my home port.

The SAMTANA had to dry dock over Christmas and this gave me a fortnight at home. So I did a foolish thing, I decided to stay with her for another voyage. The Superintendent had assured me she was going away for only two months. This was all the qualifying sea time I needed for my 1st Mate's ticket. Instead we were away for eleven months! I can remember little of this voyage, except that we were in the middle of the Pacific Ocean when 'V.J. Day' was declared and we were able to switch on our navigation lights for the first time since war broke out. Also remember having a good time in Charleston U.S.A where the locals made a great fuss of us. We got 2 days extra pay for 'V.J. Day' – £2.34! We paid off in Swansea on 26th November 1945 and I went ashore for 3 months leave (unpaid) to study for my 1st Mates certificate. One studied hard in those days because of the shortage of money. With a brand new 1st Mates certificate, I signed on another 'Liberty' ship this time the SAMAUSTRAL. This voyage was longer than the last, 12 months and 28 days. I was 2nd Mate with Chas. Sutherland as 3rd Mate who I was to sail with later in the Cairn Line. I forget most of this voyage except that once again I was in Calcutta when the Hindu and Muslim fanatics were slaughtering each other. We were moored at buoys in the River Hooghly and we were able to watch hundreds of bodies floating past as the dead were dumped in the River. We all thought that we were going home from Calcutta. Instead we were diverted to Adelaide in Australia where we had a marvellous time. At last we headed for the U.K. arriving in London and paying off on 21st May 1947. I was soon off again this time 'signing on' a 'Glasgow Tramp', the S.S. DORNOCH. This was a short voyage to Lagos in West Africa returning to Hull on the 20th August 1947. This gave me enough 'sea time' to qualify for my 'Masters Certificate' ticket. I passed for this first time on the 20th December 1947. I say first time, because many of my fellow students didn't. I got my ticket just before the arrival of a new examiner, dreaded Captain Sargeant, who seemed to enjoy failing everybody who came before him. With a brand new 'Captains Ticket' I weighed up my position. 26 years of age I was a stranger in my own home town, still living with my Mother, no money, no girlfriend, so I decided to look for a shipping company, which would bring me home more often. I was lucky that a vacancy occurred in the Cairn Line for 2nd Mate, at this time. This was a small Newcastle Shipping Company with only three elderly ships, but it was much sought after and I was lucky to get in. So on the 21st January 1948, the day after I had received my Certificate, I joined the CAIRNAVON (IV) as 2nd Mate. Here I found my old ship mate Chas Sutherland was 3rd Mate. I made one happy voyage to Canada in this ship and would liked to have stayed there. Unfortunately Mr Eric Cairns himself came aboard and offered me the 1st Mates job on a sister ship the CAIRNVALONA. He must have been amazed when I told him I wasn't very ambitious an didn't want to change, but he insisted and off I went to Leith to join the older of the three Cairn Line ships. Though I was very proud of my first ship as Chief Officer, she was 30 years old and looked it. She also had rod and chain type steering gear, which went out before the war started. This, the steering gear, gave me a lot of trouble, the chain frequently breaking, always in bad weather of course. The CAIRNVALONA carried 12 passengers and I felt sorry for these poor people. They were accommodated in six cramped cabins with narrow bunks and only one bathroom. Two of the cabins were situated on the starboard side of the lower bridge and just getting in and out of them could be hazardous in rough weather. There was no bar, no armchairs, the only place they could gather was the ships saloon. They had to put up with this for fourteen days in some of the worst weather in the world. Gales, fog, icebergs, the voyage must have been a shock for many of them. Their first impression of the ship must have been quite a surprise. They inevitably arrived when the ship was taking coal bunkers in Leith Docks and we were buried in coal dust. The CAIRNVALONA had to take extra coal aboard and this was stored in temporary wooden boxes built around the funnel. Added to this we had to take 200 tons of ballast on deck. So the old ship was not a pretty sight and I remember at least two elderly ladies who wisely changed their minds and abandoned ship before we sailed. I had only been two voyages in the CAIRNVALONA when I was asked to take over as Captain for one voyage only! From 2nd Mate to Master in six months! I was only 27 years of age – very young to be Captain and a lot of people didn't like it. My sudden promotion had been brought about by Captain Monlineux sudden departure. With the confidence of youth I took over my first (and last) command. I never bothered about a Captains uniform or cap with the scrambled eggs – it was only going to be for six weeks. I had requested that Chas Sutherland, my old shipmate from the SAMANSTRAL and CAIRNAVON (IV) be transferred to my ship as Navigator and this was granted. I never asked Sutherland what he thought about it, but I think he enjoyed the trip we had made together. It was different in as much as we called in at Quebec en route to Montreal for the first time. We had a lot of fog but I was able to keep going and we had a quick turn around and we were back at Newcastle Quay in record time. Handed the ship to her new Captain G.R. Norvell.

Norvell was lucky in that the ship was now fitted with radar. This made a huge difference in navigating in the ice and fog on the Canadian run. Settled back in my role as 1st Mate and stayed with Norvell for 22 voyages running Newcastle Quay, Leith to Montreal in the summer and St John N.B. in winter. This meant I was home every five weeks for about a week – an ideal life after years of tramping round the world never knowing when you would be home. Apart from the usual foul weather nothing much happened in these three years. I remember while the floor of the pantry situated amidships was being repaired the shipyard workers uncovered a 20ft long split in the main deck. This opening ran halfway across the breadth of the ship and could have led to the ship breaking in tow in extreme weather. This was soon strapped up and we carried on.

Another episode – I had returned from leave and was watching my ship entering Leith Lock. Approaching the lock the Pilot had used the port anchor approaching the lock. We then loaded whisky, embarked the passengers, and prepared to sail. Sounding round the bilges before departing the Carpenter reported the bilge pipes were full at No2 hold. Sailing was cancelled divers arrived and found a huge gash in the ships hull caused by the ship 'sitting' on her anchor. This led to a long spell in dry-dock during which time I met the girl who was to become my wife. I had been three and a half years with the Cairn Line, but felt I was getting nowhere. There were two new ships being built but I got the message that they were bringing in new men for these, and my prospects of promotion were nil. Also, now courting madly I wanted to get closer to Edinburgh.

CAIRNVALONA

I was determined to get back to the U.K. – Canada trade for the reasons aforementioned and applied to' Donaldson's of Glasgow, a famous old Scottish firm. I doubted they would take on a 'Sassenach' so was surprised to get a 2nd Mate berth on one of their liners, the converted 'Victory' ship LAURENTIA. This ship plied between Glasgow and Montreal docking in Glasgow every 21 days in the summer and cruising to Vancouver in the winter. She had been converted to carry 70 passengers and had a speed of 15 knots. Coming from rigours of the Cairn Line this was like paradise to me. A week in Glasgow every month when we were all went on leave. Then a week at sea, a week in Montreal, another week at sea and back to Glasgow. We sailed to a schedule set out each year and we kept strictly to departure and arrival times. All I did was stand the 8-12 watch, assisted by an apprentice and a quartermaster who served tea and toast from a silver tea service. I had left the CAIRNVALONA on 17th August, 1951 and was back at sea on LAURENTIA on 23rd September 1951. I had a very pleasant fifteen months on LAURENTIA getting married during this time.

Marriage puts a different approach to life and I had to accept that there was no chance of promotion in Donaldson's and my £12 per week wage wasn't enough. I decided to take a giant step downwards and transfer from Cargo liners to N.E. Coast Colliers. Without home trade experience, I was lucky to get a Mates job in the S.S. HUDSON BANK. This was quite a culture shock switching from general cargo and passengers to coal cargoes with all the accompanying noise and dirt. I enjoyed the life, however, being in contact with home on a weekly basis. I enjoyed the East Coast navigation, you were always in close company with other ships, buoys, lightships etc - never a dull moment. We worked 'four on' and 'four off' watches, which gave us a lot of overtime so my wages had shot up to the princely sum of £15 per week, more than I earned deep sea. Worked much harder for it though. Sometimes we loaded at Blyth and sailed the same day, and the occasional weekend in our home port was a luxury. We were one of the few ships at sea during the big storm of January 1953. Fortunately we were running before the wind, bound from Hull to the Thames. Even so I remember being 'pooped' by a wave as high as the funnel-curses from the engine room as solid water entered the engine room skylight. We arrived in the Thames to find Canvey Island under water, as well as several of the jetties.

With Blyth as our home port, I was in touch with the Pilots and learned that they had a vacancy. In the past they had only accepted shipmasters as Pilots but the earnings were poor and they were prepared to take me. I had always fancied pilotage since my first voyage. This, and being newly wed, made me jump at the chance and I was duly accepted as a very junior Blyth Pilot in December 1953. I paid off the HUDSON BANK on 13th November 1953, thus ending my seafaring career, after almost 16 years. A hard, lonely and miserable life, when you were always saying goodbye to friends and relations. Financial rewards were nil as well. I kept a record of my earnings at sea and found that I had only earned £4000 for the whole period. I remember getting married on the strength of a £60 pay-off from LAURENTIA.

After eleven months at Blyth I was able to secure a position as River Thames Pilot, transferring to London in January 1955. I was there until my retirement in January 1987. During this time I witnessed the sad demise of the British Merchant Navy and to Pilot a British ship became a rare event.

N.E. Forth

WAR MEDALS AND COMMENDATIONS NEEDHAM EDWIN FORTH MASTER MARINER
1939 - 1945 WAR MEDAL
1939 - 1945 ATLANTIC STAR
1939 - 1945 STAR
1939 - 1945 ARTIC EMBLEM
1940 - 1945 AFRICA STAR & BAR
1941 - 1945 BURMA STAR
1943 - 1945 ITALY MEDAL & BAR

(7m). **Charles SUTHERLAND** - Master Mariner.

In August, 1939, Charles started his career as a Cadet with J.C. Harrison of London, serving on board the HARDINGHAM, and other ships during W.W.II. In 1944, he passed his 2nd Mate certificate.

He joined the Cairn Line of Steamships in 1947, as 3rd Mate on CAIRNESK (III) with Captain Ian Grant Foster as Master. Later he joined CAIRNAVON (IV) as 2nd Mate, with Captain A. Henderson as Master. In 1948 Captain J. W. Scott became Master.

In 1950, Charles was appointed 1st Mate on CAIRNAVON (IV). In 1951, Captain George Percy became Master. Charles passed his Masters certificate in 1951, and thereafter rejoined CAIRNAVON (IV) as 1st Mate.

Sailing home from Port Churchill in the usual bad weather the Captain asked him to check the forepeak hatch. Whilst doing so, along with a Cadet and the Bosun Charles Warriner the vessel shipped a heavy sea and Charles was thrown against the windlass. He sustained a fractured left leg and his left ear was nearly severed. When the wave hit, the Cadet was also swept off the fore castle head and washed along the deck amidships. He was extremely fortunate in being able to pick himself up without a scratch. The Bosun was however washed over the side, but managed to cling onto the rail, suffering a badly sprained shoulder. Taken amidships from the forecastle head by the 2nd. and 3rd. Mates, Alan Fairley and Norman Shell, Captain Percy and the second mate saw to his injuries, placing the leg in a splint and stitched the left ear back into place. The Cyprian Chief Steward hovered in the back ground muttering all the time "I don't like the look of this" Nobody did, particularly Charles! The CAIRNAVON (IV) sailed to Greenock, River Clyde, and Charles was taken to hospital. The registrar attended to his leg, after which he was about to leave, when Charles asked him about his ear. The registrar took one look and said there wasn't anything to be done as Captain Percy had done an excellent job!

Charles left the CAIRNAVON (IV) to join the CAIRNESK (III) as 1st Mate in 1956. In March of that year, the CAIRNESK (III) was badly damaged in a gale, and Charles obtained photographs of the damage at St Johns N.F.

Later in 1956, Charles relieved Captain J.W. Scott on the CAIRNDHU(IV) as Master. In 1957. he was offered and accepted a position as Marine Cargo Surveyor and Assessor with the Newcastle firm, F. B. West Co. Ltd. Charles sailed 61 voyages with the Cairn Line.

CAIRNESK (III) - Gale damage, March, 1956

DGE-A lifeboat on port and starboard sides unshipped. NO 1 HOLD-several hatch

BRIDGE – A lifeboat on port and starboard sides unshipped. NO 1 HOLD – several hatchboards stoved in. No 2 HOLD – Derricks unshipped. FORWARD MAST HOUSE – Vents sheered off at base. FORWARD PORT BULWARKS – 35 feet sheered off. SALOON PORT HOLES – Glass smashed. ACCOMMODATION – Amidships flooded. FOREMAST LIGHT AND CARRIER – Sheered off and missing, situated 86 feet high above sea level.

(7n). **Jack E. LENHAM** - Master Mariner.

Jack joined the Cairn Line on 4th November,1942, as a first trip Cadet, serving onboard the EMPIRE SAILOR in Liverpool, Her cargo included phosgene gas shells and canisters of mustard gas. The Master was Fred Fairley. Only 17 days after joining, the EMPIRE SAILOR was sunk by UB-518 with the loss of 23 crew. (*Section 5r-Alan Fairley reports on the EMPIRE SAILOR*).

In January, 1943, having been repatriated from Halifax. N.S. on the ANDES, he joined the CAIRNESK(III) (Master, Captain E. A. Organ) remaining till 1946. Sailing 16 trips across the North Atlantic, Jack thought, it was excellent training in seamanship, no time for navigational training. A rough trade in tough times with may hair raising experiences. "In those days it was all great fun".

Later Jack gained his 2nd Mates certificate at Nellists Nautical College, joining H. E .Moss Tankers for 2 years.

The next 6 months were with MacAndrews Line, and then he joined the Vestry Group (Lamport & Holt, from 3rd Mate to Master) where he remained for 43 years before retiring.

Jack became Marine Superintendent in the West Indies, for Lamport, Booth and Blue Star Lines for 8 years. Moving to New York for 2 years, before returning to Liverpool, still as Marine Superintendent. Later he became Manager Cargo Handling and Port Operation for the Blue Star line. In his last year, he was appointed Chairman of Liverpool Steamships Owners Association.

Jack though the Cairn Line was not a bad place to start, and they did have some characters – Captain Organ and Andy Guild B.E.M. the Bosun.

WAR MEDALS AND COMMENDATIONS
JACK E LETHAM
MASTER MARINER

1939 - 1945 WAR MEDAL
1939 - 1945 ATLANTIC STAR
1939 - 1945 STAR

(7o). **John LUKE** - Master Mariner.

John was appointed a Cadet on 21st March, 1944 with R. C. Chapman & Son, manager of combined company of Carlton S.S. Co. & Cambray S.S. Co. Ltd. He remained until 5 July 1949 onboard the MERTON (I).

In 1944, on a voyage from Swansea to Canada, the MERTON (I) struck an iceberg. A tug and frigate escort towed the ship to St Johns N.F. The MERTON (I) then travelled to Sydney,Cape Breton Island, where a block of several tons of cement were placed in the bows – then onto Quebec and Montreal to discharge her cargo. She returned to Quebec to dry dock, where a new bow was fitted.

In January, 1945, whilst in a convoy, from the U.K. to Canada, in fog, the MERTON (I) lost contact with the convoy. She sailed on in foul weather, somehow lost a pintle off the rudder, taking 33 days to reach Halifax N.S.

On 11th April,1946, John transferred to the OTARU, which was the first British ship to sail from the UK to Japan after W.W.II. They had loaded a cargo of salt in Egypt-cost 60/- (£3) a ton.

MERTON (I)

During one voyage – 3 weeks into the voyage, an A.B. died and was buried at sea. They reached Belfast, then onto Avonmouth, before the widow was informed. She did not receive any monies from the date the A.B. had died.

Note: There were several similar cases, throughout the war-where was the compassion or Justice?

John joined the CANFORD as 3rd Mate-Anglo Swiss Maritime-sailing to the Mediterranean in 1949. Later that year John sailed on the ETHEL EVERARD, until 13th October, 1949 as 3rd Mate.

WAR MEDALS AND COMMENDATIONS
JOHN LUKE
MASTER MARINER

1939 - 1945 WAR MEDAL
1939 - 1945 ATLANTIC STAR
1939 - 1945 STAR

Between 1951 and 1953 he sailed as 3rd and 2nd Mate on the CAIRNAVON (IV) (ex EMPIRE SNOW) (George Percy as Master).

Later John sailed as 1st Mate on the OAKLEY, 2nd and 1st Mate on the ACCUM, then 1st Mate on the THOMAS HARDIE and CAPITOL. The last four ships were North Thames Gas Board Vessels, John sailing with them from 1954 to 1959.

John was then appointed in charge of 'laid up tonnage' at Hartlepool until September 1959. He then became a Trinity House Pilot in the North Channel based at Harwich, working the ports of Felixstowe and inwards to the Medway Gravesend and Harwich, finally retiring in 1988.

(7p). **William Peter WALLACE** – Chief Officer

Bill joined the Merchant Navy in 1945, serving as a Cadet on CAIRNESK (III). Later he gained his 2nd Mate certificate, sailing as 3rd Mate with the Court Line, on the WELLINGTON COURT. Bill then took up a position as 2nd Mate with the Currie Line, onboard the HORSA.

WELLINGTON COURT.

HORSA.

Bill rejoined the CAIRNESK(III) as 3rdMate. In 1952 he then joined the CAIRNGOWAN (IV) as 3rd Mate on it's maiden voyage. In 1953 he gained his 1st Mates certificate, and in early 1954, joined the CAIRNDHU (IV) as 2nd Mate in Middlesbrough. Unfortunately, he had to attend hospital for an operation and had to sign off, through a diabetic ailment.

He immigrated to Montreal, Canada, married Margaret Howie,and they had two daughters named Sandra and Beverly. He became a naturalised Canadian Citizen, and retired in 1994, but sadly died in 1996.

(7q). **David Muir AITCHISON** - Master Mariner.

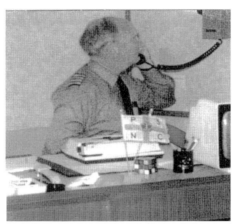

Master on ' OROYA' in 1984.

David was born on 24th March, 1928 in Newcastle-upon-Tyne. He joined the Merchant Navy on 27th August, 1945, placed on the Merchant Navy Reserve Pool as a Cadet. Transferred to FORT DEARBORN. 7,150grt. (built by Burrard, Vancouver) for Ministry of War Transport and managers by Haldin & Phillips for Court Line. On 12th March 1946 he was admitted to a hospital in Port Said. On 4th April,1946 he shipped out on the TILSINGTON COURT to Birkenhead. Between 10th May, 1946 and 27th December 1947, David served on the UFFINGTON COURT until 20th September, 1947, as Cadet and thereafter as 3rd Mate.

Between 20th August, 1948 and 30th March, 1950, David served as 3rd Mate onboard the SINNINGTON COURT. On 22nd December, 1950, David joined as 3rd Mate on the CAIRNVALONA until 26th June 1952, at which time he transferred to the CAIRNDHU (IV) still as 3rd Mate, however, he became 2nd Mate on 2nd August, 1953. David became 1st Mate of the CAIRNDHU(IV) on 14th August, 1955 and remained until 20th January, 1960.

Between 1 February 1960 and 9 June 1965, David served as Master (20 times) and 1st Mate (21 times) on various Cairn Ships, namely CAIRNGOWAN (IV), CAIRNDHU (IV), CAIRNFORTH, CAIRNAVON(IV) and CAIRNGLEN (III) – (mini bulker).

David was engaged in serving as Master (17 times) and Chief Officer (20 times) between 26 August 1965 and 29 November 1972 on the following ships: MANCHESTER FREIGHTER, MANCHESTER ENGINEER (III), CAIRNGOWAN (IV), LANCASTRIAN PRINCE, MYSTIC, SOMERISLE, MEDIC, PENNINE PRINCE, LAURENTIC and COTSWOLD PRINCE.

After 1972, there are no further records within National Archives, Registry of Shipping and Seaman and Maritime Coastguard Agency. However, Mrs Audrey Aitchison gifted the photographs of David as Master on the OROYA, which shows him onboard in 1984.

Audrey has also said that before David retired, he had been Master on three ships of the Furness Withy Line, carrying cargo of equipment, stores etc. to Stanley in the Falkland Islands, for delivery to the airport.

The following were gifted by Mrs Audrey Aitchison:

1.   CAIRNDHU(IV).   Launch on 9th. April, 1952.

1.Launch of CAIRNDHU(IV).

2..CAIRNDHU(IV) : Leaving Hartlepool for sea trials.

CAIRNDHU(IV)   On trials, passing Old Hartlepool, (At stern). The
                                'Heugh' Lighthouse can be seen at the rear of the
                                Mid-ships deckhouse and No. 4 hold.
                                Newspaper Article by Peter Anthony.

3. CAIRNGOWAN (IV) QUAYSIDE.

Peter Anthony

One of the oll "Cairns", berthed at Newcastle Quay-side. The year: 1952.

Reminder of the past

IN THE days when ship spotting from Tynemouth or South Shields pier could be a full-time hobby, one of the most familiar markings to be seen was a black and red funnel with two white bands and a white triangle between them.

Seeing those markings the knowledgeable river-sider would know that the vessel's name began with "Cairn"; that it was one of the cargo liners of the Cairn-Thomson Line sailing regularly between North-East ports and Canada under the management of Cairns, Noble and Co., of Newcastle.

Changing patterns of shipping brought the close-down of the line and the familiar funnel markings vanished from the river scene.

But I am happy to report that this little bit of Tyne shipping history is still evident on the high seas.

The huge Furness Withy shipping group which took over Cairns, Noble has transferred the familiar funnel markings to a fleet of small bulk carriers trading on voyages like Bordeaux - Manchester or Trondheim-Rotterdam.

The "family" name survives, too, with vessels like the Cairncarrier, Cairn-leader and Cairnranger.

Good to see that a big faceless corporation like Furness Withy is romantic enough to preserve some part of the old links with the days when Thomas Cairns started business as a shipbroker in the firm of Starks and Cairns and was joined a few years later by William Joseph Noble.

(7r). **Alan FAIRLEY** - O.B.E. -
Master Mariner.

Alan always wanted to go to sea. In 1946 as a schoolboy in Montreal he had the opportunity during his summer vacation to sign on as an assistant steward on the Hudson Bay Company's R.M.S NASCOPIE. In fact Alan's interest in the sea was soon recognised by the Captain who allowed him to work with the deck crew whenever possible.

The Ship was to make her annual voyage to the company's trading posts in Eastern Artic and the Hudson Bay. She sailed from Montreal on 6th July, 1946 and visited twenty outposts, steaming over 10,000 miles before returning to Montreal, 3 months later, on the 3rd October. 1946.

On board the trip, in addition to the Hudson Bay Company's personnel, were Inuit who had been receiving medical treatment in Montreal, members of the Royal Canadian Mounted Police, an Anglican and a Catholic Bishop, three U.S. Naval Officers and a medical team to carry out medical examinations of the native people at the various outposts. The ice was particularly heavy in the eastern Hudson Bay that year and at one stage the ship was icebound for over a week. The farthest north the NASCOPIE reached was Dundas Harbour on Devon Island, which had earned the title of being the most northerly post office in the British Commonwealth. In fact the post master travelled with the ship but faithfully took all the mail ashore for franking before returning it on board to satisfy stamp collectors from all over the world.

This voyage was to be NASCOPIE's last to the High Arctic, as on her next annual voyage she foundered after striking an unchartered rock at Cape Dorset, Baffin Island. This voyage set the seal for Alan's future career.

July 1947 saw Alan joining the CAIRNESK (III) in Montreal as Cadet. His fellow Cadets at the time were Bill Wallace, John Baxter and Bill Tinkler. Captain I. G. Foster was Master and Tommy Hands was Chief Officer. (The latter commanded corvettes during the war and later became Harbour Master of Tees and Hartlepool Port Authority). Stanley Wilkinson was Chief Engineer and Andrew Guild B.E.M was Bosun. In 1950 during his final year of cadetship Alan was promoted to 3rd Officer. He had done well in the annual exams set by the Merchant Navy Training Board being awarded their certificate of Merit and Bronze and Silver medals in each of the three years.

In 1951 he gained his 2nd Mate's certificate sailing with the Port Line for two years on the MANZ Line service on the PORT QUEBEC. He later sailed on the following Port Line ships. PORT WYNDHAM, PORT VICTOR, PORT DUNEDIN and PORT LINCOLN. He rejoined the Cairn Line after qualifying for his 1st Mate's certificate serving as 2nd Mate and Chief Officer on CAIRNESK(III), CAIRNAVON(IV), CAINRDHU(IV) and CAIRNGOWAN(IV).

In 1956 he passed for Master and was the last Chief Officer of the CAIRNESK(III) before she was sold and renamed

PORT QUEBEC entering Sydney Harbour.

ZERMATT. Coincidentally his father, Fred Fairley had been her first Chief Officer on her maiden voyage in 1926.

Alan then spent two years in Canada as Cargo Superintendent for Furness Withy. His main function was overseeing the loading and discharging of Manchester Liners and other vessels for which Furness Withy were agents in Montreal during the summer and in St John N.B. in the winter months.

He returned to the U.K. in 1959 and after two voyages as Chief Officer of Trinder Andersons AJANA Furness invited him to take over as Managing Director of Tyne Stevedores, a company that they had acquired in the Tyne. He also managed a Rigging Company and a firm of cargo surveyors, which Furness Withy had also purchased.

In 1972 seeing the rundown in the British Merchant Fleet, Alan applied for and was appointed Operations Manager for the Port of Tyne Authority. Within a year he was offered the post of Commercial Director and membership of the Board.

Port of Tyne.

In 1983 he was appointed Managing Director a post he held until his retirement on 21st November, 1997 (which happened to be the anniversary of the torpedoing of one of his fathers ships, the EMPIRE SAILOR). Previously he had been appointed O.B.E for "Services to the Shipping Industry".

R.M.S NASCOPIE

(7s). **Donald GOLIGHTLY** - Master Mariner.

LA LOMA

LA SIERRA

BALUCHISTAN

KOHISTAN

In 1949, Donald joined the CAIRNESK (III) as a Cadet, and later served on CAIRNGOWAN(IV). Later he was 3rd Mate on the CAIRNESK (III). He then served in Buries Markes Co. on LA LOMA (Ex.SAMSTURDY) as 3rd Mate, and on LA SIERRA as 2nd Mate.

Later he moved to the Frank Strick Line, serving on BALUCHISTAN as 3rd, 2nd and 1st Mate, and also as 1st Mate on KOHISTAN. He left in 1970 and became Assistant Harbour Master in Blyth, Northumberland.

(7t). Derek MILBURN - Master Mariner

Presentation: Mrs. D. MILBURN and Captain Derek MILBURN. 1977.

Derek joined the Merchant Navy in December, 1949, serving as an apprentice with the Trader Navigation Co. and later as 3rd Mate with them. He joined Prince Line/Furness Withy in May, 1955, serving in various vessels in their fleet. In 1972, he joined Shaw Savill's motor vessel LAURENTIC as 1st Mate and later with the Cairn Line as Master of most of the mini bulkers.

In November, 1959, he passed the M.O.T. Masters Foreign Going Certificate, gaining the highest marks for the masters certificate in that year, and in February, 1960, the Merchant Navy & Airline Officers Association presented him with the 'Griffiths Award. for this achievement. In 1983, Derek was, along with many other officers, made redundant.

WAR MEDALS AND COMMENDATIONS
DEREK MILBURN
MASTER MARINER

1977 MEDAILLE DE BRONZE
(SOCIETE NATIONALE DE SAUVETAGEEN MER)
COMMENDATION FOR BRAVERY IN RESCUING CREW
OF SHIP IN DISTRESS - 'VERIC'

List of Ships.

CAIRNRANGER.   Mate
LONDIS.   Mate
SWIFT ARROW.   Master, January 1975
COTSWOLD PRINCE.
CAIRNTRADER.
CAIRNROVER.
CAIRNLEADER.
CAIRNFREIGHTER.
CARNOAK.
CAIRNFREIGHTER*   collision anchored flushing roads (see report)
CAIRNASH.
CAIRNFREIGHTER.
CAIRNFREIGHTER.
MALVERN PRINCE.
CHILTERN PRINCE.
CAIRNFREIGHTER.
COTINGA.
CAIRNCARRIER.

The following documents are also included:

1.   Sample of port calls: They show quite a punishing itinery.

2.   Report of rescue from Derek MILBURN.

3.   Map – Position of rescue.

4.   Award: Medaille- de- Bronze'

5.   Report of collision of 'CAIRNFREIGHTER' by 'AL RAHIM'.

6.   Photographs:
           (a) ESSEX TRADER'– [Fotoflite] – 5th June, 1953.
           (b) 'LAURENTIC' – [John Clarkson] – 14th November, 1972.
           (c) 'MALVERN PRINCE' – [John Clarkson] – 1981.
           (d) 'LONDIS ' (As' ATLANTIC BERMUDIAN ') – [John Clarkson.] – 1974.

Port	Arrive		Depart		
1982	**m.v. Cotinga**				
Middlesbrough	Join 18.1.82		18.1.82	1700	
Maaloy	23.1.82	1350	24.1.82	2028	
Mo I Rana (Norway)	26.1.82	1052	29.1.82	0518	
Tyne	1.2.82	1845	4.2.82	0705	
Goole	5.2.82	0548	6.2.82	0318	
Lowestoft	6.2.82	1850			
		Left vessel 8.2.82			

Port	Arrive		Depart		
	m.v. Cairncarrier				
Calais	Join 15.2.82		17.2.82	1830	
Brunsbuttel	19.2.82	0940	20.2.82	0700	Engine trouble
Ventspils anchor	22.2.82	1100	22.2.82	2340	
Riga anchor	23.2.82	1705	(Ice bound)		
Riga	10.3.82	0408	12.3.82	0030	
Kiel Canal		14.3.82			
Hamburg	15.3.82	0034	15.3.82	1650	
Bremen	16.3.82	0642	17.3.82	1730	
Brunsbuttel	18.3.82	0500	18.3.82	1515	Bunkers
Ventspils anchor	20.3.82	1200	26.3.82	1600	
Riga anchor	27.3.82	0824	15.4.82	2322	
Riga	16.4.82	0200	20.4.82	0400	
Gefle (Gavle)	21.4.82	0924	22.4.82	1654	
Nordenham	26.4.82	1124	27.4.82	1500	
Hamburg	28.4.82	0405	8.5.82	1600	
Kiel Canal		8.5.82			
Holtenau	9.5.82	0420	9.5.82	0824	
Malmo	10.5.82	0045	12.5.82	1454	
Porsgrunn	13.5.82	1215	13.5.82	2124	
Ymuiden	15.5.82	1630	18.5.82	0230	
Dordrecht	18.5.82	1154	left vessel 18.5.82		

Port	Arrive	Depart	
1983	**m.v. Aeneas**		
Tilbury	Join 1.2.83	3.2.83	
Antwerp	4.2.83	5.2.83	
Brake	6.2.83	7.2.83	
Bremerhaven/ Bremen	9.2.83	Left vessel 13.2.83	

END OF SEA SERVICE

@ Shaw Savill Line A Member of the Furness Withy Group

Shaw Savill & Albion Co Ltd

m.v. "Cairnleader"
At sea, bound Glomsfjord,
30th March 1977

Shaw Savill Line,
The Marine Manager,
Marine Office,
Royal Albert Dock,
London E16 2BR.

Rescue of crew from yacht "VERIC"

Dear Sir,

At 0010 hours 29th March, a red light was sighted two points on the port bow, by the lookout Mr R.Wheatley, E.D.H. at a distance of about three miles. The master was called to the bridge and course altered towards the sighting. The general alarm was sounded and extra lookouts posted. Ten minutes later a red parachute distress signal was clearly seen, followed five minutes later by a second. At 0025 the yacht was spotted through the glasses and the whistle sounded, searchlight switched on to indicate we had seen them

At 0035 we were able to manoeuvre close alongside the yacht and get some lines attached, which was not made any easier with the weather conditions at the time, a fair lee was made however, with both ouselves and the yacht rolling heavily and seas sweeping our hatches. At that time she was just abreast our No.2 hatch on the port side. On our port roll, the first three people, two men and one woman managed in turn to jump on board aided by my crew. Unfortunately the yacht drifted off and fell astern under our port quarter before the other three could manage to jump. We had lowered mooring ropes aft but the other girl grabbed one of them and was pulled of the yacht into the sea. With considerable difficulty the two remaining men managed to grab hold of her arms and pull her back on board over the transom and we managed to get the yacht back to abreast No.2 when the remaining three literally dived on board. The yacht was then cast adrift. I would expect it to have sunk pretty soon afterwards, as she was being damaged when alongside us, the mizzen mast being nearly collapsed, and of course she was shipping seas into the cockpit all the time and I saw little point in standing by her until it did sink.

At 0115 hours we proceeded at slow speed in the general direction of the Gironde river. I inspected all the survivors, who were all in severe shock, but with very little wounds, the girl who was in the sea having miraculously not even a rope burn. When the captain of the yacht had recovered sufficiently to give me some details, I contacted Bordeaux radio on M.F. and asked them to give the information to the French athorities and transmit a navigational warning. The yacht captain also spoke to the shore operator for a few minutes, he also had no injuries.

The chief officer dressed all the wounds and they were all put to bed and made as comfortable as possible. One of the girls was completely exhausted having been sea sick since they left La Rochelle on the Saturday.

We arrived at the Gironde faiway buoy at 1600 hours on the 29th but the weather was still too rough to anchor. Pilot boarded and we arrived off Le Verdon and anchored at 1818 hours.

The port doctor and harbourmaster boarded, and after a brief examination all left for shore at 1845 hours, in good spirits. We weighed anchor at 1900 hour and resumed passage full away at 2048 hours, 29th for Glomsfjord.

I would like to commend my crew on their unfailing courage, without regard to their own safety, during the rescue, and apart from there being up to the waist in water most of the time, I am happy to say there were no injuries. I was made to understand from the harbourmaster that some sort of recognition would be made to the ship from the French athorities.

135

As a matter of interest, the yacht was a nine metre job, two masted and painted
a blue/green colour. She only had one set of sails, which were carried away,
no radio transmitter and the engine had broken down. The radio receiver batteries
were also on the way out, so it was lucky they had distress signals. All six
were making their first ocean passage, and from what they told me, it would be
their last. They were all aged 20 to 24.

If we had been in ballast condition I fear that some or all would have
perished and by the grace of God we were in the position we were, having been
more or less hove to all day. They were bound for Santander, having hired the
yacht for one week for about £250 and 1000 francs deposit.

Position at time of rescue 44 36' N., 2 36'W.
Weather:- Good visibility, wind NExN force 7 Rough sea, mod/heavy N'ly swell
Names of survivors:- Armelle BOURSEAU
                      Nadine BENICHOU
                      Denis BENICHOU
                      Francois LECHAT
                      Michel RENAUD
                      Marc GANEM

Yours faithfully,

Master

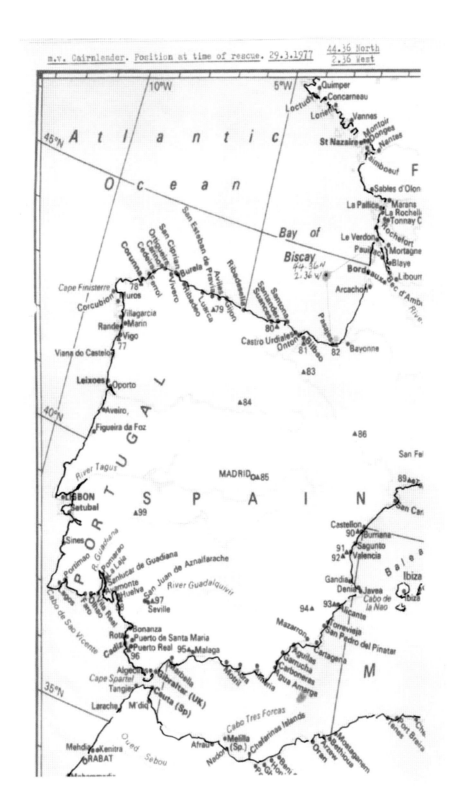

SOCIÉTÉ NATIONALE DE SAUVETAGE EN MER

9, RUE DE CHAILLOT, PARIS (XVIᵉ)

MÉDAILLE DE BRONZE

au captain D. MILBURN
pour le sauvetage des passagers du voilier
français "Véric", le 29 mars 1977.

Paris, le 19 JUILLET 1977   L'AMIRAL, PRÉSIDENT DE LA SOCIÉTÉ

LE SECRÉTAIRE DU CONSEIL D'ADMINISTRATION

SHAW SAVILL & ALBION COMPANY LIMITED

14/19 LEADENHALL STREET, LONDON, EC3V 1NP

DAMAGE REPORT (DECK & ENGINE)

(Confidential Report for the information of Company Solicitors)

(d)

SEE PAGE 30

Four copies to be completed—one to be retained on board, and at first port of call three copies (for Marine Manager, Technical Manager and P & I Department) to be forwarded to Marine Manager, Shaw Savill, Marine Office.

N.B.—Any collision with another vessel or stranding, salvage services received or rendered should be reported by letter addressed to "The Solicitors", c/o the Company, together with copy of completed Damage Report.
An immediate telephonic report must be given to the local branch office or Agent as soon as practicable.

STEVEDORES DAMAGE TO SHIP. Procedure as detailed in "Master's Instructions" to be carried out and copy of completed "Stevedore Damage Form" to be attached to this report.

SHIP CAIRN FREIGHTER VOYAGE 57 REPORT NO:- 57/1

PART I.

MASTER'S REPORT   30-9-78

Date and time of occurrence (G.M.T.): ~~0~~ 0446   Place of occurrence: FLUSHING ROADS
(Local Time) 0646   Ships Time 0546

Account of Accident. V/L anchored to 7 shackles on port anchor in Flushing Roads. At 0544-0545 AL RAHIM observed crossing close ahead from port to starboard and closing. Engines put full astern. 0546 AL RAHIM struck bow with his starboard side 1/3 length from bow of AL RAHIM

SKETCH:

|←——— 23' ———→|

Deck Rippled →

Bulwark Rail

ELEVATION VIEW OF BOW   PLAN VIEW OF BOW

Damage sustained, giving precise location (if Shell damage—indicate whether Port or Starboard). Please state clearly whether Plate Nos. counted from forward or aft. (The terms 'stem' and 'stern' are not to be used.) If damage to cargo involved, brief details and stowage:

Fo'c'sle bulwarks and brackets crushed at bow. Port mooring fairlead dislodged, starboard fairlead bent ...

139

If vessel deviated to effect repairs
Details of deviation, additional bunkers consumed at sea and in port etc. ........N.O............................

Damage done to other property:

Estimated cost of repairs: £........................

_____   Chief Navigating Officer
             or
            Chief Engineer Officer .... Master

                   30-9-78 Date

Extracts of Logs (where appropriate) to be attached.

_____

PART 2.

SUPERINTENDENT'S REPORT (This part to be filled in by the Master/Chief Engineer if Survey and Repairs effected abroad, and/or when no Superintendent in attendance.)

Surveyed by: .... representing Underwriters

     MR KARELSE

                                  "   Classification

                                  "   Owners

                                  "   Third Party

Port.....FLUSHING.............

Date ....30. 9. 78.............

Estimated cost of complete repair.......N.T KNown.£

State below brief details or repairs effected:—

                                                CONTRACTOR

     Temporary ....
                   NONE
             ....

         Cost (estimated or actual)................................£

     Permanent (part or complete) ....
                   none
            ....

         Cost (estimated or actual)................................£

     Deferred ....
        CERTIFICATE OF SEAWORTHINESS FOR 3 MONTHS
        ....

         Cost (estimated) ....£

If Ship's personnel engaged on repairs, full details to be given on separate sheet.

Spares used from Ship's stock: ....None...............................
(Full details to be given)   ....
                       ....

Period vessel detained (if any): ....
Seaworthy Certificate issued by:........L.R.S. BY Mr KARELSE................
If Seaworthy Certificate Conditional, give details......REPAIRS TO BE EFFECTED WITHIN THREE MONTHS.
....

.... 1. Master, Superintendent (or Master if appropriate)

Diagram showing the movement of vessels prior to and at the time

of contact with the AL RAHIM.

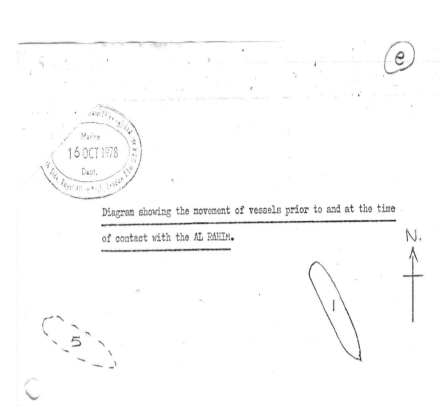

WIND. →   ← TIDE.

Cairnfreighter swinging
approx 20°
either side of
this heading.

CAIRNFREIGHTER.   C.F.

AL RAHIM   1,2,3,4,5,

This diagram has been compiled from information received from
Mr. T.J.W. Wilson, Second Officer.

141

ESSEX TRADER.   [Fotoflite].

LAURENTIC.   [J.Clarkson].

MALVERN PRINCE.   [J.Clarkson.]

LONDIS. (as ATLANTIC BERMUDIAN).   [J. Clarkson].

7U. : **JAMES CUTHBERT WHINSHIP.** – Chief Officer.

I was born on 15th December, 1932, at Houghton-le-Spring, County Durham. In 1949, I enrolled at the South Shields Marine School and on 26th October, 1949, joined the S.S. CAIRNESK(III), as a Cadet. I was to complete ten voyages, altogether, on that ship. On 10th/11th December 1950, I had an accident on board the CAIRNESK, while at sea. On arrival off Leith, I was transferred by lifeboat ashore and conveyed to Leith hospital for treatment to head injuries that I had received in a fall, during 'heavy weather', off the East coast of Scotland. My injuries were not 'life threatening', as I only stayed in hospital for a few days, before being discharged and returned to the CAIRNESK, which was still discharging in Leith Docks.

I left the Cairn Line on 17th April, 1951 and joined the Blue Star Line as a Cadet.

Between the 25th of June, 1951 and 2nd July, 1952, I served on the TASMANIA STAR, on the Australia / New Zealand run. I then joined the NELSON STAR and between the 17th August1952, and the 6th February 1953, on the same run. I sailed for three voyages, one of them on charter to the Australia – Asia Line, running between Singapore/Malaya/ Sumatra /Java and Russia.

NELSON STAR.

I gained my Second Mate's Certificate in June,1954, and as Third Mate, sailed on the NELSON STAR (4th March,1955 – 19th January,1956), then joined the WELLINGTON STAR. (5th March,1956. – 3rd, February, 1957). Two voyages on each ship.

On the 9th August, 1957, I gained my First Mate's Certificate and sailed as Second Mate on the ARGENTINA STAR. (6th September, 1957-28th October, 1957), between South America/Spain and Portugal. I then sailed for two voyages to South America and Italy as Second Mate onboard the NAPIER STAR.

ARGENTINA STAR.

On the 6th of January 1958, at Newcastle-upon-Tyne, I married my wife Catherine.

I left the Blue Star Line on the 23rd December, 1958 and gained employment in a shore position with the Newcastle City Council rates Department, Newcastle-upon-Tyne.

On the 5th November 1961, I sailed as Second Mate on the motor vessel PUKEKO. on her 'delivery voyage' from Greenock on the River Clyde, to Auckland, New Zealand. Built for use in the New Zealand coastal trades, her owners were Richardson & Sons, of Napier.

Later I became employed in dairy farming in the Thames area of New Zealand, but that only lasted for six days, my 'shortest job ever!' I then gained employment with the Revenue Department of Auckland City Transport. I later joined another local company, New Zealand Forest Products Ltd., in Kinleith, North Island, as the laboratory manager, dealing with 'quality control. I was with them from April 1962 until December, 1979. I was residing then at Tokoroa. In December 1979, I left 'Forest Products Ltd' and went to live on Waiheke Island – as a 'Beachcomer'.

In the 1980's I sailed as First Mate, for one voyage, on board THE SPIRIT OF ADVENTURE a brigantine training ship, manned by an all girl crew!

On 12th September 2002, I returned to my present residence at Tokoroa, where I still live with my wife and spend most of my spare time playing snooker!

(7v.) **Neil GILLENDER** - Fourth Engineer.

NEIL and JOAN
"Wedding day"

Neil joined the Merchant Navy in 1951, serving with Shaw Savill on the RUNIC and FORDSDALE. During 1952 and 1953 he served on the CAIRNGOWAN (IV) from 6th to 4th Engineer, latterly with various "home trade" companies.

Neil left the Merchant Navy in December, 1954, and thence gained experience in the coal and steel making industries before embarking into the power generation field with consulting engineers (Merz and McLellan).

He joined British Gas (Northern) in 1968 as a Project Engineer and retired in 1990 as Construction Engineer in charge of the design and installation of high pressure gas installations.

At the time of retirement Neil was a full Chartered Engineer with the "Institution of Mechanical Engineers" the "Institute of Gas Engineers" and the "Institute of Energy".

FORDSDALE

RUNIC

(7w). **Alastair J. ANDERSON** - First Mate

Alastair joined the Merchant Navy in 1952, as Cadet onboard CAIRNESK (III) and also on CAIRNGOWAN(IV) under Captain Ian Grant Foster. He later joined Border Tankers. He returned to the Cairn Line, serving on CAIRNFORTH and CAIRNGOWAN(IV).

He left after 10 years, taking up a shore job, first in France, Cyprus, Florida and then in the U.K. Alastair is a proficient yachtsman, sailing the Atlantic three times. Once with a friend on his yacht 'RAPTURE' and twice as skipper with crew on 'SMUGGLER' a 72 foot yacht.

Anchorage of Saint Honorat Isle.

RAPTURE. Built in 1977 by Endeavour Yacht Corporation. (Hull No. ENC321871276. Sail 470 sq feet. Ballast 5.300lbs. Disp. 11700lbs.) *Note: The author spent 10 days sailing the Mediterranean. Skipper-Alastair, Bosun-Author, AB-Scott.*

Berthed in Mariner Camille Rayone,
Golfe Juan near Canne.

In 1955, Alastair was a Cadet along with Ken Hunter, Rodney Vincent Park and Donald Young (Youngy). Master was I. G. Foster, 1ˢᵗ Mate-Jack Lobban, 2ⁿᵈ Mate-Alan Fairley, 3ʳᵈ Mate-Alan Stanton and Radio Officer-E Johnston.

I. G. FOSTER   E. JOHNSTON   Alan STANTON

Jack LOBBAN   Alan FAIRLEY

ALASTAIR REMEMBERS THE FOLLOWING INCIDENT, INVOLVING "THE BUGLE"

We were tied up in Freemantle and opposite us, on the other side of the river was the British India cadet ship CHINDWARA with about 50 cadets on board. We were very proud of our flag routine, prompt 08.00 hrs, 3rd Mate would blow a whistle and the flags would be hoisted or broken out as was appropriate. The CHINDWARA went one better than us and had a bugle sounded instead of the whistle. We were not happy about being out done and decided that something must be done to rectify the situation.

We did careful reconnaissance of the procedure the CHINDWARA cadets went through and established that the bugle was kept in the chartroom at the rear of the wheelhouse. How to get on board unobserved was a problem. They had two cadets as night watchman on the gangway but cargo nets were over the side of each hatch. There were Samson posts, with ladders, adjacent to the bridge port and starboard.

It was late at night, I think we had all been ashore drinking, when we decided that we would raid the CHINDWARA and get the bugle. With the dory that we used for painting the side we rowed over the river to the CHINDWARA under cover of darkness. Our plan was to throw a line up over the side and climb up, not a hope! Next we landed on the quay and decided that the best way up would be by the cargo nets. I think Ken Hunter and I were the only ones to go on board. I remember that Ken put his foot into an open port hole as we were climbing up but it didn't disturb any of the sleeping cadets. I was up the Samson post and onto the wing of the bridge like a shot. The chart room was just behind the wheelhouse and the windows were like the old railway carriage windows, lift up and push out. It was too easy and I couldn't believe my luck when I put my hand through the window and found the bugle. It had a lanyard so I hung it round my neck and was off back down the Samson post, across the deck and over the side by the cargo net. Ken followed behind me but he got hold of a phone cable, which gave way as soon as he put his weight on it. He made a hell of a splash when he landed in the harbour. Park at this time was in the boat with 'Youngy' and, fearing that Ken may have hit the quay on his way down, dived in and swam towards him at a fast crawl. Ken surfaced saw this thing coming towards him and thought it was a shark and was prepared to fight for his life. Ken was not injured and they both got back into the boat and we were back across the harbour to the CAIRNGOWAN.

The next morning we watched with great amusement as they frantically searched for the bugle and eventually had to settle for a whistle.

A day later we were sailing to go east around the coast and had to swing. As our stern swung past the CHINDWARA, Park, who could play the bugle, blasted out with the "waltzing bugle boy". I was on the wheel and Jack Lobban turns to me and says "do you know anything about this Anderson", "no sir not me". After a lot of formal protests we had to return the bugle but we still had the tale to tell.

(7x).   **Peter WALLACE** - Master Mariner.

Peter joined the Merchant Navy in 1953 as a Cadet on CAIRNESK(III) (Captain George Norwell) and CAIRNGOWAN (IV) (Captain Ian Grant Foster).

In 1957, he gained his 2nd Mate Certificate and joined PORTSLADE as 2nd Mate, then Manchester Liners turbine steamer, MANCHESTER CITY as (3rd Mate).

1958.   He rejoined CAIRNGOWAN(IV) as (3rd Mate).

1959.   Peter gained his 1st Mate Certificate.

1960.   He joined the CAIRNFORTH as (2nd Mate)

1962.   He joined the CAIRNDHU as (2nd Mate).

1963.   He joined the CAIRNGOWAN (IV) as Chief Officer, and then CAIRNDHU as (2nd Mate).

1965.   'Super Cargo' on SCHIAFFINO FRERES and later on the CAIRNAVON(V).

1966.   Peter gained his Masters Certificate and joined MANCHESTER ENGINEER,
          CAIRNGOWAN(IV) and MANCHESTER FREIGHTER (CAIRNFORTH), all as
          Chief Officer.

1967.   Peter retired and entered the business world.

SCHIAFFINO FRERES   WORLD SHIP SOCIETY

MANCHESTER ENGINEER (ex CAIRNGOWAN(IV)) FURNESS WITHY GROUP

MANCHESTER EXPORTER (ex CAIRNDHU (IV)) FURNESS WITHY GROUP

MANCHESTER FREIGHTER (EX CAIRNFORTH (IV)) FURNESS WITHY GROUP

Peter recalls the following voyage involving the CAIRNESK (III) in March 1956:

Westbound on the last winter voyage of the season we sailed from Grangemouth for St John N.B. with a good cargo of general. Usual winter North Atlantic weather but at about 40° West things turned bad, with mountainous seas and precipitous swell the ship pitching and rolling violently, shipping seas over decks and hatches and spray overall. The steering gear was in constant motion and an inspection showed that the tooth sections on the steering quadrant were working loose. The engineers rode the quadrant and secured the bolts holding the tooth sections in place. The Master, J. Hogg, decided we should only have three helmsmen working two on and four off, the two oldest Cadets and an experienced AB were closed . The storm was moving slowly as was the ship. The seas grew higher and higher and of course the ship was hove to waiting for things to improve. At about five bells in the forenoon watch the Master, 3rd Mate and Cadet (P Wallace) saw a monster wave directly in front. Amazingly the ship rose up and over but there was a hole behind the wave and another giant dead ahead. As we crashed down into the trough the wave broke under us and I saw it come over the top of the fore mast and it crashed into the bridge.

As we came out the other side we could see the devastation on the fore deck through the remaining wheelhouse windows. No 1 hatch was stove in, the bulwarks on the port side as far aft as the shrouds had gone as had the multi-directional vents on the mast house. The derricks were a mess, No 2 port was athwart- ship behind the winches the other three were held up on the toppings lift, and charged about as the ship rolled, endangering the mast and top mast. Port holes within the saloon were broken and the bridge was missing most of its port and starboard wings and part of the wheel house. The radio aerials were down and the starboard life boats had been lifted in board against the half deck house bending the davits to suit their new position. The deck cargo of steel plates were loose, sliding about causing damage to the deck fittings.

The most pressing problem was the derricks. Two very brave men, the 2nd Mate (Ian Gault) and an A.B. of his watch went on the fore deck and cast loose the topping lift to drop the derricks. Amazingly, the ship had not suffered any structural damage to the very strong hull, apart from a split frame in the engine room. We rode out the tail of the storm and proceeded to St John, Newfoundland, for repairs.

During the days of the storm all departments had their problems, cooking very difficult, so it was tea and sandwiches. The firemen and trimmers had to travel through the shaft tunnel then move the coal to keep the steam up. The deck crew had to try and keep everything lashed down and when possible repair no 1 hatch cover. The radio officer had no radio and of course the catering staff had passengers to look after. The injuries to the crew were very light: bumps, bruises, strains etc.

We spent some time at St Johns while repairs were done. Then on to St. Johns N.B. to unload then reload, and back to Leith. When we paid off, the insurers paid us all a bonus. The two men who went on the fore deck were paid a double bonus, they were worth every penny and more.

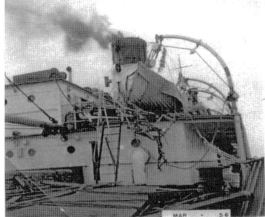

Photographs showing damage to the CAIRNESK (God bless her)

(7y). **George BURDON** – Chief Engineer.

George joined the Merchant Navy in 1953 and joined the Ben Line's steamer, BENVORLICH and then the Prince Line's OAKMORE and AFRICAN PRINCE.   Later he joined the CAIRNAVON(VI) as 2nd Engineer. He remained 2nd Engineer with Pacific Steam Navigation Company serving on their ships, FLAMENCO, PACIFIC UNITY and PACIFIC NORTH WEST, later joining Johnson Warren's CONSUELO.

In retirement he continued his enthusiastic support of all things connected with Tyneside, composing several songs and poems.   He has recorded a number of compact discs. Titles including   "When Shipping was King" and "Strands of Youth" *(See Cairn Line Song in Chapter 3).*

PACIFIC UNITY

(7z). Neil HINDMARSH – Third Engineer.

In April 1954, Neil joined H.E. Moss of Liverpool as 4th Engineer on the motor tanker LUCELLUM, the crew being flown to the ship in Rotterdam. It was a horrendous baptism, five months in the Persian Gulf on a terrible ship with continuous engine problems. Neil returned home and paid off in Greenock, Scotland.

In October, 1954 he joined the CAIRNGOWAN(IV) in Leith. The ship was on a winter charter to New Zealand, most enjoyable and a great crew. In 1955 returned to the usual trips to Canada (summer) but then went on another charter, this time to Australia.

Neil continued to sail on CAIRNGOWAN (IV) on several more voyages to Canada as 3rd Engineer. Later Neil developed a medical problem and was admitted to Newcastle General Hospital for seven weeks. Unfortunately the doctors advised Neil to stay "ashore", however, he managed 'stand by' on the CAIRNESK (III) and CAIRNAVON (IV). Shortly afterward Neil left the Merchant Navy.

[See entry regarding the football team of the CAIRNGOWAN (IV).]

(7aa). <u>**Peter REDSHAW**</u> – Third Engineer.

Having served my apprenticeship at C A Parsons Heaton Works in engineering and obtained deferment from entering into H M forces I decided at the age of 22 years, I would join the Merchant Navy. After making some enquiries I decided that the Cairn Line a Newcastle company would be just right, homeport every seven weeks sailing to Canada.

I contacted the Cairn Line and was asked to visit the office at Milburn House in Newcastle for an interview.

I was accepted and told that I would be joining the "CAIRNESK" as 5th. Engineer, £32.00 per month all found, when she arrived in the Tyne and due to go into dry dock.

My uniform was purchased at Wm. Wood & Sons, Ocean Road, South Shields. Almost everyone bought his or her uniforms from Woods, as they were uniform specialists for all the services.

Having now signed on at the Mercantile Marine Office in Newcastle, I had officially entered the Merchant Navy, complete with my "Seaman's Record Book and Certificates Of Discharge" document, which included a photograph of myself. This document, for which I paid the pricely sum of 2/6d, would remain with me as a record of the ships on which I sailed, and I still have it some fifty years later.

The CAIRNESK was late in arriving and I was summoned to join her at Newcastle Quay on 31st. December 1955, New Years Eve about lunchtime.

Arriving with my holdall and some of my belongings, I was met by the 2nd. Engineer, who showed me to my cabin, introduced me to some of the other engineers. Every one was in haste to get home for the holiday.

I was told that I would be duty engineer tonight and as the donkeyman, greaser and fireman on watch would look after things below, I was not to worry. Later I went below to talk to the donkeyman, hoping that all was well I turned in.

Most of the crew had gone home, either to their homes locally; the Scottish lads had gone home for Hogmanay. It was customary for the Scottish element of the crew to stand by whilst the ship was in an English port and vice versa. This was a great understanding and worked very well during the four years I was with the Cairn Line.

After dry-docking, we loaded some cargo in the Tyne for Saint John New Brunswick, and coal for our bunkers, then to Grangemouth, our final port of call in the UK.

In Grangemouth we loaded our final cargoes. One evening whilst in Grangemouth, the Chief, Second and myself went ashore to the Juniper Lea Hotel for a drink, as closing time in those days was 9.30 p.m. this did not give us much time to have a drink. In the lounge I happened to see some fellows I knew from Parsons, who were commissioning the Kincardine power station and as they were resident in the hotel and as long as they were buying drinks we could enjoy their hospitality.

A most enjoyable evening was had and we all returned to the ship in a taxi.

Cairnesk at No. 5 Shed. Saint John NB.

When at sea I was to be on daywork starting at 07.00 until 17.00.
The Cairnesk was a Parsons Steam Turbine driven ship. With three, coal fired, Scotch boilers. The H.P. and I.P turbines were on the same shaft, The L.P turbine was on a separate shaft, both shafts entering the double reduction gearbox, driving the single output shaft.

Built in 1926 by Wm. Pickersgill & Son of Sunderland.
Gross Tonnage 5033.49.
Net Registered Tonnage 3013.74.
Indicated Horse Power 2875.

Each watch had an engineer, donkeyman, greaser, three firemen, and three trimmers.

We left Grangemouth headed for Canada, out through the Pentland Firth along the North coast of Scotland passing cape Wrath on to the Butt of Lewis. After Lewis we headed out into the Atlantic and although the sea was calm with virtually no wind, there was an Atlantic swell, and I became very sick, suffering from the dreaded seasickness. I remember looking in my mirror and seeing this rather greenish looking person. After about thirty-six hours of not eating very much the old Chief said that I must eat! I sat in the engineer's mess that evening and ate a few dry cracker biscuits. I really enjoyed my breakfast the following morning and was never troubled with seasickness again.
Every morning it was my task to start up the engine driving the compressor for the refrigeration, initially Cairnesk had fridge cargo space, now reduced to domestic use only. The start up I did before breakfast and the engine was shut down again about mid morning or when the refrigerator temperature was sufficiently low enough.
Initially I had little part in the watch keeping duties as my work was set out for me to look after and repair the deck gear.
The winches were Clarke Chapman open type winches and were in a dreadful state, worn bearings, big end pins worn oval, leaking glands, piston rods worn, etc. I could only do the best I could with the spares available and the whole of the two-week journey from the Butt of Lewis to Nova Scotia I was on deck every day in glorious sunshine although rather cold. Not often does one see an engineer with a suntan.
Saint John New Brunswick in the middle of winter is in my opinion a very wonderful place; the Saint John River flows into the Bay of Fundy noted for its very high tides, 70ft. (21 metres).

In fact the Bay of Fundy has the highest rise and fall of tide in the world. Going ashore often meant that if you were walking down the gangplank, on your return some hours later you would be walking down again to re-board the ship.
At the point where the river enters the bay the river is restricted and this causes the river to create the falls at low tide. On the flood the river is restricted by the great flow of water into the Bay of Fundy and this creates the falls in reverse. Above the falls the river widens out into a large loch, this freezes over and the ice can be several feet thick in places. This phenomena allows the locals to entertain them selves, fishing through

holes in the ice, ice yachting, skating, I even saw private cars racing each other on one occasion.

At high tide slack water it is possible to navigate vessels through the gap into the Saint John River. In the observation centre there were photographs of vessels navigating the falls.

Any one who reads this and was in Saint John around this time will remember Garr's Diner. Fifties music, hamburgers, hot dogs, clothing for the cold winter weather, boots shoes and much more and Garr himself.

The return trip to Scotland was very similar to the voyage out, calm seas plenty sunshine, again I was working on deck on the deck machinery, the winches having done their job in Saint John with no major breakdowns. Also there was the daily routine of running the refrigerator engine. Eventually arriving in Leith 20th February 1956.

Signed off, and signed on for the next trip, the first entry in my discharge book. Captain J. Hogg and William Walker were the two signatories.

Discharging our cargo mainly grain in Leith and in the Tyne, I was settling down into a routine as 5th Engineer, (Fiver as I was sometimes called.) we left, after a brief few days at home from Grangemouth bound for Saint John. Due to the limited boiler pressure of 200 psi. which originally had been in the order of 250 psi. The old Cairnesk could only steam at approximately eight knots maximum taking about two weeks to cross the Atlantic. The Chief Engineer Mr. R. D. Oswald told me that during WWII he was on the Cairnesk for most of the duration and as she was so slow she could not keep up with the convoys travelling at ten knots. Fortunately as a straggler she was so far behind the convoy that the enemy submarines did not come near. Possibly being first home with the next convoy.

This trip the weather was so bad that I did not venture out on deck to do much work, some work on the after deck was possible, we encountered head seas most of the way across.

On the morning of the 15th March I was in the refrigeration flat starting the engine as usual and there was a large thump, and I felt the ship shake. Wondering what was happening I poked my head out of the engine flat to discover the Second Engineer, Ernie McPhee, coming up the ladders completely soaked. Asking him what had happened he told me that a wave had come over the ship and down through the engine room skylights, flooding the engine room to about waist deep; all this water drained into the bliges and was pumped away.

A message came from the bridge that the ship was to go on "STANDBY" in the engine room we doubled up on watches, Fourth with the Third and myself with the Second, four hours on four hours off.

This picture was taken a few days before the storm and everything looks neat and tidy the deck cargo all stowed and lashed down, the derricks in place and the ventilator cowling beside mast intact. The anchor winch and the hand railing the fo'csle looking as it should.

Some of the passengers we had on board were taking breakfast in the saloon when the wave hit, the saloon portholes were stove in, water and glass every where and as far as I remember no one was hurt, although rather damp.

We reduced speed heading into the seas and winds of, gale force maybe even hurricane force.

The wave that engulfed the ship did considerable damage; the front woodwork on the bridge was carried away as were the windows in the bridge. I was told that we were lucky that the funnel did not go also.

The fore deck was a shambles; a cargo of steel plates lashed down on the deck broke their bonds and was sliding about on deck, causing more damage.

The following photographs show more clearly what happened than any word can express.

These photographs were taken shortly after the storm and it had been decided that the ship would head for St. Johns Newfoundland being the nearest port to undergo repairs.

As can be seen the extent of the damage caused by the wave, displaced derricks, ventilator cowlings, and a section of bulwarks torn off the port side. The No. 1 hatch was stove in and the temporary covering over the hatch can be seen in the right hand photograph. The deck cargo unsecured, it was too dangerous to walk on the deck, what the crew did to secure what they did, was in my opinion, heroic.

The ship was approximately 800 miles East of Newfoundland when the wave hit us; the storm lasted for 48 hours. Information was received from other vessels in the area, a Norwegian ship was behind us and some of her crew was injured. We also heard that the Queen Mary some 500 miles South of us also had sustained damage to the ship and some of her passengers were injured.

The galley was in the same accommodation as the engineers; because of this we had all our meals in the engineer's mess and did not need to venture onto the deck to go to the saloon for our meals.

During the night of the same day as the storm there was another shuddering of the ship. From our accommodation on the port side we could hear activity on deck above us. .

A wave had struck the starboard side flooding the stewards' accommodation and damaging the two starboard lifeboats.

On the day after the freak wave, a call to the engine room from the bridge said that the steering gear was not answering to the helm properly. The 2nd Engineer and I went along the tail shaft tunnel and climbed the shaft to the after accommodation. To gain access to the steering flat one had to leave the accommodation and onto the deck into the steering flat. The little steam engine was working overtime first one way and then the other, it was discovered that one of the segments on the quadrant had come loose and was stopping the quadrant from operating fully in both directions. Both the 2nd and I climbed on to the quadrant and succeeded in tightening the two bolts that had become slackened allowing the segment of the gear to come out of line.
With the gears now in alignment the quadrant was free to traverse its full distance in each direction. Still sitting on the moving quadrant the bolts had to be thoroughly tightened with a ring-flogging spanner; with me holding the spanner the 2nd swinging the big hammer we eventually tightened the nuts and the lock nuts. All the other segment bolts were also checked. With all our attention on the task in hand we had not realised how violently the ship had been performing pitching and rolling, coming out on the afterdeck was to me awe inspiring. Behind us was a wall of water then seconds later the sky, as we were riding into the sea and in the trough of these huge waves. We stood for a short while watching the spectacle and swimming past us was a very large school of dolphin the adults swimming in a ring around the smaller younger dolphin. These dolphins looked to be rather large beasts but were not killer whales.
They passed us very quickly and it was back down below, along the tunnel and report to the chief the problem. In these seas it was impossible to travel too fast, I believe we were reduced to approximately two knots, sufficient to give steerageway.

I was interested in photography, and had with me my Paterson developing tank, printing paper, contact printing frame and developers. In the few days before arriving in St Johns I developed the film and made some contact prints. These were shown to the skipper and upon arrival in St. Johns I took the negatives to a photographer in St Johns and had some enlargements made for the skipper, Captain Hogg, to send back home to the office. The office in Newcastle were sent copies showing the damage, with the knowledge of what had been damaged, they were able to plan the repairs necessary when we returned home to dry dock in the Tyne.

During those days before arriving in St Johns the conditions on the bridge must have been dreadful with little or no protection from the elements. When we eventually reached St Johns in a snow storm a complete white out on the 20th March. I was on the lower bridge for a while looking to see if I could take any further pictures, but to no avail.

As we were entering the harbour, steam for the anchor winch for'd and mooring winch aft was required, unbeknown to everyone all the fore deck pipework had been damaged when the steel sheets had broken loose. When the steam was put on deck the whole of the fore deck disappeared in a large vapour cloud, steam was then shut off. We entered the harbour under our own steam and were assisted by the tugs.

More pictures of the storm damage taken after arriving in port. It is surprising that so much damage could be caused by one wave.

The damage to the bridge as can be seen was quite extensive

We were in St. Johns undergoing temporary repairs for about two weeks to enable us to carry on to Saint John NB. Whilst in harbour a complete new steam pipe and exhaust system was fitted to the fore deck, the original pipework was all copper with brass flanges. Good scrap value which was shared out amongst the engine room staff, I received some Canadian Dollars, do not remember how much.

During our stay the Ships Company were invited to the Merchant Navy Officers Club and were entertained by the local members on many occasions.

Eventually we left after the repairs had been done, the ship once again seaworthy and arrived in Saint John NB., somewhat later than expected. The winches did not give too much of a problem during the cargo handling, although due to the many leaking piston glands some times there was clouds of steam around the deck, much to the annoyance of the stevedores. Our cargo unloaded and the homeward bound cargo loaded, mostly grain, fully laden we set sail for home.

The return trip was, I was pleased to say was not so hectic as the outward trip. Limited amount of time on deck to work on the winches.

On arrival in the Forth we had to anchor to wait for the tide and when it was decided to enter the harbour at Leith, when passing through the lock gates we scraped the bottom of the hull on the lock sill. Arriving in Leith on the 26th April 1956 some 64 days after signing on in Leith on the 21st February. I signed on again and was told that I was being transferred to the "CAIRNDHU" and would join her in the Tyne.

After Leith it was South around the coast to the Tyne my homeport and into dry dock. The dry docking being necessary after the storm and sliding over the sill in the lock at Leith.

Signing off at Newcastle on 3rd May 1956, home for a few days leave before joining the Cairndhu,

Another steam ship this time with oil fired water tube Babcock & Wilcox boilers and Parsons Marine Steam turbines.

The Cairndhu at Grangemouth

The "CAIRNDHU" was built in 1952 by Wm. Gray & Co. Ltd. of Hartlepool.
Gross Tonnage 7503.27
Net Tonnage 4631.12
Shaft Horse Power 4650
Net Horse Power 831

I joined her at Newcastle Quayside on 14th May 1956 as 5th / Junior Engineer, There were three junior engineers, 4th, 3rd, 2nd and Chief, the Chief was Mr W G Campbell. The Captain was J W Scott.

With much to learn about the new ship, I was allocated to be with the 2nd Engineer as the other two juniors had sailed on her before and knew the vessel well. On this trip we sailed for Montreal, as the St. Lawrence River was now open after its closure during the winter months. From the Butt of Lewis to Belle Isle, about 2600 nautical miles, the entrance to the St. Lawrence, took about seven days, much quicker than the old Cairnesk.

In port the junior engineers worked watches of 12 hours on 24 hours off this gave us the opportunity to go ashore on numerous occasions.
Some friends of the family lived in Sherbrooke some miles East of Montreal and on one of the 24 hour off duty periods I visited them. Travelling on a Greyhound bus for about two and a half hours and 100 miles later I was met by them at the bus terminus. This trip was for me most exciting, seeing some of the countryside flashing past and travelling on the right hand side of the road.
After this short visit, I returned to the ship the following day to report for my next watch.

In Montreal after discharging our cargo we occasionally moved our berth to the grain silos to load grain, which was our main cargo for home.

The outward-bound cargoes were very often machinery parts, steel and also large amounts of Scotch Whisky.

Montreal is a city with a difference completely split into two. The French quarter to the East and the English quarter to the West, the divide was at a street called Bluery. St. Catherine Street the main street in Montreal with all its shops ran East and West through both areas.

Trips ashore were spent in buying presents for taking home, and visiting some of the sights.

I remained on the Cairndhu until 6th December 1956, having completed four trips to Canada and one trip round the coast to Middlesborough where I signed off, going home to get married.

After my leave I joined the Cairngowan, sister ship to the "Dhu", on the 10th January 1957 in Grangemouth. On the first trip it was Capt. J Hogg ex the Cairnesk who was the relief skipper for Captain Foster who was her usual skipper. The Chief Engineer was Mr W S Wilkinson.

I remained on the Cairngowan until 18th September 1957 during which time there was another trip to Saint John and four to Montreal. The adjacent photograph taken as we passed underneath the Jacque Cartier Bridge. Chief Engineer Mr W S Williamson bottom right.

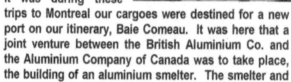

Discharging a Euclid dump truck in Montreal, little did I know that one-day I would be greatly involved with this type of equipment?

It was during these trips to Montreal our cargoes were destined for a new port on our itinerary, Baie Comeau. It was here that a joint venture between the British Aluminium Co. and the Aluminium Company of Canada was to take place, the building of an aluminium smelter. The smelter and all the infrastructure was to be supplied by the British and the electricity supplied by the Canadians. There was a large hydroelectric dam, to the north of Baie Comeau built by the Canadians and most of the mechanical equipment supplied by the British was taken out on the Cairn Line vessels. In addition to the plant, personnel were also sent out from Kinlochleven, Scotland. Many of the staff were also passengers on the Gowan and the Dhu.

Baie Comeau was at that time only accessible by sea or by seaplane. The landing area for the seaplanes was on a lake to the North of the township. The harbour consisted of a single mole, shaped to create a basin with berthing facilities on both sides but no cranes.

This photograph of the Cairngowan was taken one evening when I went for a walk having seen the hilltop from the ship. There were no tracks or paths; I made my way upward in not to densely wooded area, some of the trees had been felled, keeping the ship in view most of the time. After reaching the summit I sat on a tree stump and admired the view, taking the picture, and whilst sitting there four chipmunks arrived and quite oblivious of me sitting there scampered about looking for food. Baie Comeau is situated on the North shore of the St. Lawrence River so the photo was taken looking in a Southerly direction, looking to the North from my vantage point one could only see pine trees as far as the eye could see.

After my walk and later, speaking to one of the locals I was told that there were bears in the woods above the town. I never saw any but they may have seen me!

We visited Baie Comeau many times and on all occasions were always entertained by the local populous. There was a shortage of alcohol and because of this we could sell our docking bottle for much more than it cost us, supplementing our sub.

The voyages taking us up and down the St. Lawrence River In both the "Dhu" and "Gowan" were to me most spectacular in many ways. There was always something different to see.
One morning after entering the river through the Belle Isle Strait the smell of pine trees wafted down the ventilators into the engine room, going on deck to open the valve to fill the galley fuel tank the shoreline was one mass of pine trees in all directions.
Another time whilst entering the St. Lawrence in the early evening a magnificent display of the Northern Lights was seen, glowing green and yellow curtains hanging in the Northern sky.
In the Gulf of St. Lawrence a school of Orca swam past the ship obviously feeding, possibly on the salmon which abound in that area.
Other ports of call on the river were Sept Iles, Trois Rivieres, and Chicoutimi some 30 miles from the St. Lawrence up the Chicoutimi River. Charlottetown, the capital of Prince Edward Island, Quebec with its historic connection with General Wolfe and

Montcalm and During WWII with Winston Churchill meeting the American President Roosevelt at the Château Frontenac.
Another port of call closer to Montreal was Sorrel, here there was a heavy lift crane and on one occasion our cargo was an alternator stator casing, well over a 100 tons, from C A Parsons, my old firm.

The photograph on the left shows the Chateau Frontenac and to the right of the photograph are some cannon, these were made at the Carron iron works at Falkirk Scotland. We always visited Quebec as our last port of call after leaving Montreal homeward bound.

A closer view of one of the cannon.

It was from here that I saw the Cairavon homeward bound. The "Avon" was an Empire ship, triple expansion steamer, launched as the Empire Snow in 1940.

After leaving the "Gowan" I the rejoined the "Dhu" on 23rd September 1957 now sailing as 4th Engineer, one more run to Montreal before the St. Lawrence freezes over. This was for most of the crew a time to do our Christmas shopping.

Stock in the shops seemed more plentiful than back home and the shops were already decorated for Christmas.

Tinned "Fancy Red Sockeye Salmon" was a favourite as although salmon in tins was obtainable at home it was much cheaper in Canada. Another item was "Saran Wrap"; this item was not available in the UK at that time, later to be known as cling film, we were therefore able to use it long before it was available on the home market.

At the end of this trip I decided that I had sufficient sea time, and would attend Marine School in South Shields to take my Part "B" of my Second Engineers ticket, having been exempt from part "A" with my qualifications obtained before going to sea. I left the ship on 27th November and started the course with high hopes.
Six weeks into the course I was told that I was short of sea time by 10 days! I would not be allowed to continue with the course and could not take the examination; I asked if I could take the examination and complete the sea time afterwards. I was most disgusted with the attitude and bureaucracy that existed at that time. Things may have changed now! Perhaps not.

It was back to the Cairndhu on the 18th January 1958 in Newcastle upon Tyne, the 4th Engineers post was unavailable so I sailed as junior once more but was still on 4th Engineers salary. Another trip to Saint John and on our return to Leith all the juniors and the 4th and the 3rd were all having a drink in the third's cabin when in came a stranger, announcing himself as the new Third. No one knew that the third was being replaced and there was a deathly hush and a very angry third Engineer.

The new 3rd was another Geordie, Brian Bambra. As I was the senior junior I was assigned to the new 3rd Engineers watch, unbeknown to me at that time he lived on the same estate as me in Gosforth, Newcastle upon Tyne and as a result we became very good friends over the years.

The "Gowan" and "Dhu" were sister ships and the engine rooms were identical with the exception of the steam and exhaust valves for the afterdeck and steering gear. The valves were handed and if one was used to one vessel care was needed when operating these valves on the other ship. The inevitable happened when one junior used to the "Dhu" transferred to the "Gowan" and when leaving Montreal, late season, was sent to shut the steam off deck and shut the steam off the steering gear, resulting in the "Gowan" running aground in the St. Lawrence. The ship I believe had to be dry-docked and just missed being ice bound in the St. Lawrence at Montreal for the winter.

Both ships had Clarke Chapman totally enclosed cargo winches which were lubricated continuously and as a result unlike those on the Cairnesk, during my time on the ships I never had to work on the winches apart from checking the oil levels and topping up the oil when necessary.

One trip after leaving Grangemouth Heading for Saint John we anchored in the Firth of Forth just off Leith and loaded a cargo of explosives, which we eventually discharged in Halifax, Nova Scotia.

The cargo was discharged at anchor some distance off from the harbour. Halifax had a terrible experience in 1917 when a French munitions ship, the *Mont Blanc*, collided with a Belgian relief ship, the *Imo*. On December 6, 1917, at 9am the munitions ship with a cargo of TNT and gun cotton exploded in what was the largest man-made explosion before the first testing of an atomic bomb, and is still one of the largest non-nuclear man-made explosions.

The harbour authorities were justifiably cautious when we brought our cargo to Halifax.
After moving into harbour our cargo this time although not so explosive, was Scotland's greatest export, Whisky. I do not think that I have ever seen so much whisky at any one time, and as many Royal Canadian Mounted Police (Maritime

unloading carried on all day and into the evening. At all times the security guards were present and not one bottle went missing during the whole process.

I left the "Dhu" on 5th June 1958 to join the "Gowan" with my old position as 4th Engineer, joining her on the 14th June having had a few days at home. After one trip to Montreal I had accrued some leave time and as my wife was a teacher she was on holiday in the month of August I decided to take my leave from the 29th July. I rejoined the "Gowan" at Grangemouth, again as 4th Engineer, on the 20th August 1958 after an enjoyable holiday.

The passages across the Atlantic during my time at sea although sometimes rough were never as dramatic as my second trip to sea on the Cairnesk.

On one voyage on the "Gowan" during early summer heading for Belle Isle we encountered a number of icebergs, floating south in the Labrador Current.

Photographs of some of the icebergs we saw they do not look very large but that is only one tenth of them.

Whilst passing through this area the sea temperature dropped below freezing and in the engine room the condenser circulating water pump had a covering of snow about 1" thick, looking like a large white animal in the engine room. Whilst in the area of ice flows I was in the evaporator flat starting the evaporator when I heard a groaning, moaning noise out side the hull, as the evaporator room was adjacent to the hull, this I found out was ice flows (growlers) grinding along the ship side. The first time I heard this I thought something was coming in through the ship's side, quite an alarming experience.

On another occasion homeward bound on the "Gowan" there was a storm in the North Atlantic so Captain Foster decided to head South to miss the weather, we headed so far South that it became very warm and I believe the we were only 100 miles North of the Azores. There was speculation amongst the engineers and others, that we would go through the English Channel to Leith, in fact we came up the West of Ireland and through the Minch to Cape Wrath and home along the North coast of Scotland, our normal route.

On at least two occasions in Montreal before loading our cargo of grain the ship had to be fumigated. The senior officers were accommodated in one of the hotels in Montreal; some of the crew and myself were allocated to the Stella Maris.
The fumigation usually took twenty-four hours to complete; we were back on board around lunchtime, having had a cooked breakfast. We later found out that those in the hotel did not receive breakfast.

On the 14th November 1958 I signed off and signed on again as 3rd Engineer on the following day.

On the trip round to the Tyne I was on deck whilst entering the Tyne. There is a thrill about entering your homeport and the following photographs show us entering the Tyne from the North. Seeing familiar sights and the people on the pier looking towards the ship, reminded me of the many times I had done the same thing, waving to the ships, often the wave was returned from the mysterious persons on the passing vessels.

ships, often the wave was returned from the mysterious persons on the passing vessels.

The North Tyne Pier with Tynemouth Priory on the skyline to the right of the pier.

Crossing the bar.

North Shields fish quay, fishing trawler and the High Lights.

Tyne tug coming alongside.

My wife and I had discussed the matter of me coming ashore in the near future as our first child was due towards the end of April 1959 and it was decided that I should complete this trip and retire from the sea at the end of February 1959.

Once more to Saint John with greater responsibility in the engine room and also for all the electrical machinery and equipment on board, with the exception of the bridge navigational equipment and the radio, for which the Radio Operator (Sparks) was responsible.

On the outward passage knowing that we would be at sea for Christmas I started to prepare some 15-watt pygmy lamps by dipping them in various colours of paint obtained from the ship's carpenter. Hanging them up to dry in my electrical store. With all the lamps and cabling wired up I tried them out in the Engineers alleyway, one morning whilst everyone was asleep. All was ready for the return trip if we did not get home for Christmas, it did not seem likely.

The decorations, which I had prepared earlier, were hung in the Engineer's alley tied to the pipework and plugged in to one of the light fittings early on my watch on Sunday 21st December. Much to the surprise of the Chief and the Second when they saw the lights, after breakfast it was customary for the skipper to inspect the ship every Sunday and on seeing the colourful lights in our accommodation asked who did this, and all he said was, "Very Festive". The engineers were the only people on board to have some form of decoration for Christmas.

I had heard that Christmas at sea was usually celebrated with a feast second to non. Our cook who made the most wonderful bread, also prepared for everyone a marvellous spread for Christmas Day, which was enjoyed by everyone on board.

We arrived in Leith on the 27th December having had Christmas dinner somewhere close to the Cape Wrath. Everyone having missed Christmas at home was anxious to get home for New Year. When I went on watch at midnight, I spoke to the 2nd Mate on the bridge to find out whether we would catch the morning tide at Leith on the 27th at our current speed. It was touch and go he said but if we could have a bit more speed we may make it, so I started to increase the speed by opening up the main stop valve. The tide was with us and by the time we were in the Pentland Firth we were doing 21 Knots. When the 2nd Engineer came on watch at 04.00 he had heard the engines opened up during my watch and opened her up fully.
The "channels" is a term used by all sailors; it is an expression of the excitement within oneself of coming home to port and in particular a homeport. I think most on the "Gowan" this trip had the "Channels".

The extra speed saw us catch the tide, if we had not we may have had to anchor off for a few days and probably missed the New Year.

I was at home for twelve days returning to the ship when she arrived in Newcastle on the 9th January 1959. One more trip to Saint John this one was a quick one, Leith to Leith, was six weeks arriving in Leith on the 8th February.

During this trip outward bound there was an earth on the switch board which I tried to locate and having checked all the circuits, there was only two which I had not drawn the switches to test for the earth. One was the Radio and the other was the Gyrocompass, I told the Sparks and he was adamant that there were no earth faults on his equipment. I rechecked all the other circuits and still had the earth being indicated on the switchboard, at a time when I knew the radio was not being used I drew the switch and the earth still remained. It was obvious to me that the problem was with the Gyro, I drew the switch and the earth disappeared. I immediately reconnected the switch but with the loss of power the Gyro had failed and required 48 hours to readjust. The sparks was non-to pleased, and I was told not to pull the Gyro switch without informing the bridge. Strangely enough the earth fault disappeared.

I enjoyed my experiences in the Merchant Navy, and on Monday the 9th February I left the Cairngowan and rejoined C A Parsons, but that is another story.

(7ab).   **Michael WRIGHT** – Cadet.

Michael joined the Merchant Navy in 1959 and served with the Cairn Line, on CAIRNDHU(IV),under Captain G. Percy and CAIRNFORTH. (Captain J. Hogg). During his time on the CAIRNDHU (IV) Michael recalled a boiler blowing up in Mid- Atlantic, becoming stranded and using an improvised sea anchor for several days. The boiler was made good, and they sailed to Liverpool.

Years later Michael received substantial monies from the under-writers, along with other members of the crew for their efforts in securing the safety of the ship and 'keeping the Dutch salvage tugs at bay'.

On a winter trip to Canada, he experienced snow blindness for a short period so before sitting his 2nd Mate certificate his eyesight was tested (lantern) but unfortunately he failed the eyesight test. On leaving the Merchant Navy he entered the construction business.

(7ac). **G. T. SMITH** - [C/Eng. / F.I.Mar.Est.] - Chief Engineer.

George and Milly at Buckingham Palace, 1981

He joined Associated Humber Lines Ltd (British Rail/ Ellerman's Wilson Line) as 3rd Engineer in 1959 in BYLAND ABBEY. Joined M.V. YORK in 1963 as Chief Engineer. Joined MELROSE ABBEY/BOLTON ABBEY in 1968 as Chief Engineer. The company closed down in 1971 and after a spell with British Rail at Harwich. he the joined Shaw Savill's managed Cairn Line of Steamships as Chief Engineer in 1973.

M.V. CAIRNRANGER	6/11/1973. to 5/9/1974.	Chief Engineer
M.V. CAIRNROVER.	8/12/1974. to 7/1/1977.	Chief Engineer
M.V. CAIRNFREIGHTER.	25/4/1977. to 5/5/1977.	Chief Engineer
M.V. CAIRNLEADER.	20/5/1978.	Chief Engineer

Applied "Finished with Engines" in 1981.

After retirement in 1981 Mr and Mrs G.T. Smith were invited to a Garden Party at Buckingham Palace on the nomination of the Worshipful Company of Master Mariners for Services to Shipping.

'CAIRNROVER' engine room.

The following correspondence is listed as follows:

1.   The stranding of the M.V.CAIRNROVER   1975
2.   The hazard of flow in bulk mineral cargoes.   1976
3.   M.V. CAIRNROVER on charter to Mathiesen
4.   H.M.S MANSFIELD – Tours of duty.(including Convoy HX. 229)
5.   M.V. CAIRNLEADER at Wilhelmshaven.

The Stranding of the MV Cairnrover

The Cairnrover had loaded zinc concentrate and lead concentrate at Trollhattan in Sweden for Antwerp in Belgium. When 'Full-away' I retired to lay down for a while. and in what seemed a short time the vessel came to a stop so quickly that my head was forced to the bulkhead quite strongly. I realised what had happened and raced up to the bridge where I found that the officer of the watch had mistaken a light-buoy and ran us on to the rocks. The engines were put astern but we were hard and fast but of no avail. Unfortunately the weather was bad with the wind blowing at force 8-9 and we sat there grinding on the rocks. The weather was so bad and we were so near the rocks that it was impossible to get tugs or rescue services anywhere near us so for two days at least we just sat there grinding at the rocks. As soon as the weather had moderated a diver appeared to have a look at the damage. Meanwhile I had used my invention, the 'Isograph' to make a perspective drawing of the underside of the hull and the diver was able to mark on this the exact positions of the damage which was fairly extensive. It was then decided to send out lighters to part-discharge the cargo and two tugs to stand by. These tugs were called 'Gertrude' and 'Herbert' unusual names for Swedish tugs. The Swedish customs became most interested since No 3 fuel tank was ruptured and eventually sent out what was supposed to be special gear for taking oil out of damaged tanks. They were unsuccessful and thereafter kept a beady eye on us for oil spills Once lightened enough for us to float Gertrude and Herbert towed us back to the berth for discharge, the customs following us every inch of the way as the fuel was still a serious problem. The fact that we were a British vessel, chartered to a Swede and trading in Sweden didn't help matters. On arrival at the discharge berth I promised that I would pump the oil into road tankers if they were prepared to take a little water in the last load. The top of the No3 fuel tank air-vent was removed and a fairly rigid neoprene pipe of small enough outside diameter to go down the air vent and since the fuel in the tank was floating on top of the water that had entered, we able to pump oil from near the surface with the transfer pump discharge and transfer it to deck and ashore to the tankers. Pumping via the usual suction pipe would simply have pumped water from the underside of the oil. The customs still followed us closely all the way back to dry-dock.

The above is the heading of an article written in the editorial 'Safety at Sea' in January 1980 by Warren Springs Laboratary, and refers to a British ship carrying a cargo of lead and zinc concentrate from Sweden to Belgium. The ship was in fact the MV Cairnrover.

The fact that the vessel survived is unique with this type of cargo hazard and there are facts in the overall situation which account for this survival. The loading of the lead and zinc concentrates was started at 0700 on the morning of the 31st December 1976 with two cranes. It was noticed on arrival that the lead was covered by tarpaulins but the zinc was unprotected. The lead, about 900tons, was going into No1 hatch and the zinc, about 1300tons, into No2 hatch. There were heavy falls of snow on the day before loading, but the Moisture Content Certificate showed a content well below transportable maximum.

Loading went well and the vessel sailed at about 1900 on the same day. It must be stated here that the vessel was not fully loaded due to the maximum allowed draft in operation for lake Vanern and the ship canal.

The vessel arrived at the pilot station at about noon on 1st January 1977 and proceeded to sea in a slight SW sea and swell on the Port beam. By the time that the vessel altered course at Hanstholme at about midnight the wind had increased and the vessel was pounding moderately into wind and sea on course for Antwerp.

At about 0800 on the 2nd Jan and some time after steaming into heavy sea and swell, it was noticed that the vessel had taken on a pronounced list to Starboard. All tanks, ballast, oil and bilges were sounded and, all being normal, the hatches were inspected and this revealed that the cargo was liquifying and moving over to starboard. Taking advantage of the reduced draft ballast tanks were adjusted and the shore-side authorities warned. We asked for a port of refuge and were given Esbjerg, who were willing to accept the risk and from then on we remained at abandon-ship stations, had we not been able to move ballast and had we then been subject to a beam sea the total capsize was inevitable but with good management ant with lifeboats and tugs standing by ashore we were able to make Esbjerg at about eight knots with a minimum of the pounding which is a contributory cause of cargo liquidisation. The next crisis arose when abreast of and ready for the turn across the sea to Esbjerg and at this time all were at abandon-ship stations wearing life-jackets. Almost miraculously the sea eased and we were able to make it alongside in the port of refuge.What had been one advantage was that the Rover had a substantial fore and aft bulkhead at the fore end of No1 hatch but it was horrifying to see at sea the cargo crawling like a huge monster through the lightening holes of this bulkhead. Another obvious advantage was that the vessels of this company were extremely well-found, all officers were very experienced and fully qualified. In the words of the analyst at the port of refuge : the salinity of the water content was below the salinity of drinking water.

Showing the funnel of CAIRNROVER after the Charterers, Mathiesen, attached their own house flag:

(which stands for Eric Thun A/B Lind Koping Sweden). I George Smith personally forbade them, at all costs, from placing this motif in the front of the Cairn Line of Steamships House flag.

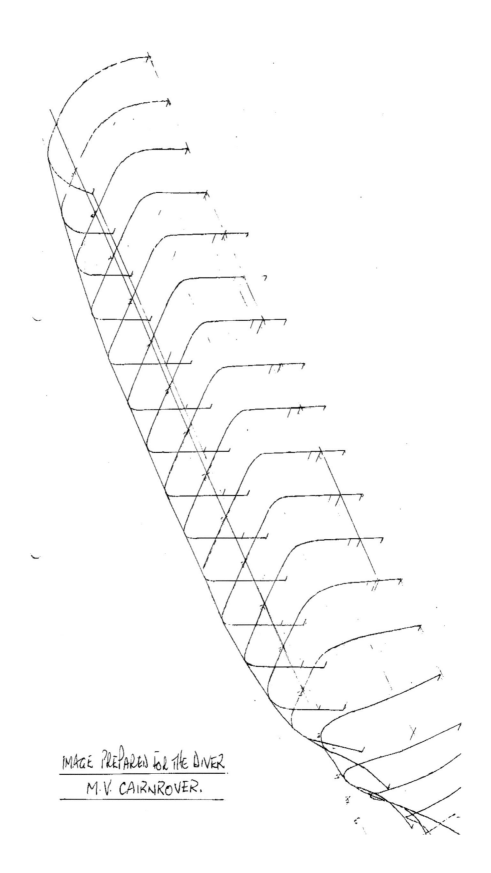

IMAGE PREPARED FOR THE DIVER.
M.V. CAIRNROVER.

176

Cairnrover discharging cargo while stranded

Photographs show Cairnrover in Esbjerg. Surveyors said that the water could be pumped from the top of the cargo but ships officers, who had been carrying out their own tests of moisture content disagreed as did company surveyors so eventually all the cargo had to be discharged. This became a lengthy undertaking since bad weather, snowfalls etc, delayed the removal of the necessary machinery. Eventually all cargo was removed and the vessel continued trading

Mr Speedy, test for moisture content.

Mr Speedy consists of a cast steel cylinder with a screwed on cover in which is fitted a pressure guage. A measured amount of the cargo is put into the cylinder, a measured amount of Calcium Carbide, the cover with pressure guage is screwed into place and the cylinder given a thorough shake. The volume of gas generated is relative to the moisture content of the cargo and the pressure registered gives a positive indication of that amount.

George wrote the following article regarding his Royal Navy Career during WWII. It relates to tours of duty onboard H.M.S MANSFIELD, whilst serving in the Mediterranean and North Atlantic, including the infamous convoy HX.229.

1939 turned out to be a year of expectation and hope particularly on the part of the elderly who could view the situation with experience and maturity.

We at the Shipyard were at an age of decision, being almost at the end of our apprenticeship. Were we to be reserved if the worst happened, or were we exempt?

In June 1939 a 35ft bride-deck motor cruiser, M.V. HILLCREST, built by my father's firm at the Timber Pond, had been completed and was to be delivered to Liverpool via Leeds and Liverpool Canal. It was arranged that I would do the trip for experience. The canal at that time was all locks and long tunnels. At Wigan there were 25 locks with a pound between each.

At one of these was a policeman who came aboard and spoke with Father, after which I was bundled below and locked in the fo'c'sle. At the next lock the policeman departed. On being released I heard that a boy of ten had been lost for days and the police had come to remove the body from the water. At my age I wasn't allowed to see a dead body. We didn't know that within two years I would be in the North Atlantic aboard an over-age destroyer involved in a savage war with U-Boats.

We arrived in Stanley Dock in Liverpool on the day that MAURITANIA sailed for trials. The HILLCREST was later commandeered for naval duty by the Admiralty.

War was declared on 3td. September and soon another apprentice Colin Wilburn and I were called up to serve in the Navy. A rude awakening indeed as we passed through the London Blitz on our way to Chatham.

We were eventually drafted to H.M,S MANSFIELD, an ex-American four funnelled destroyer. On our first commission we steamed north-about through the Pentland Firth and to the Azores to take on bunkers. The brand new crew were of course still a little green so all the time it was training and practice, fire and damage control and gunnery and torpedoes. We also had the job of pumping up the air tanks of the torpedoes.

Our next port was Gibraltar where we stood by for the famous 'Ohio' convey, named Operation Pedestal. On arrival at Gib. we had to take part in the sweep of the straits to keep it clear of mines and U-boats. We managed a night or two ashore and I was amazed and probably a little proud that walking along the high street in Gib. was like walking along Boothferry Road in Goole; there were so many Goole men on the various ships RN and Merchant. The convoy eventually departed for Malta; if this one didn't make it, it would be the end for Malta and its associated fronts.

We weren't very far into the Med. when the Aircraft Carrier H.M.S EAGLE was torpedoed and we had to stand by. We missed the convoy, which in the event arrived safely. We went back to Gib. with survivors then home to Liverpool with some of them.

After a refit in Liverpool we were loaned to the Canadian Navy and sailed for Halifax, Nova Scotia. The U-Boats on the eastern seaboard of North America were having what became known as a 'Happy Time' since Admiral King of the U.S.A would still not believe in our convoy system.

H.M.S MANSFIELD became the leader of a Canadian Escort Group and our run was from Halifax or St Johns Newfoundland. We went to 35 degrees West then escorted another convoy west-bound to St Johns or Halifax. After this, south to Boston, USA, following the same triangular route all the time except for emergencies.

Awful weather; if it wasn't Atlantic storms it was fog on the Grand Banks. The waves were so enormous that although MANSFIELD was 310ft long we would lift over the crest, then run downhill into the trough. When the bows hit the bottom of the trough the whole ship would flex and bend. The back- end where we lived, would come down in three huge bumps. This happened on every wave. On one occasion MANSFIELD left an east-bound convoy off Iceland in order to screen a contact. This took us North up Denmark Straits. Before long we were in storm force north-easterlies and a temperature of 30 degrees below freezing.

Ice began forming on all stays, guns and direction finders but much more serious was the steering wires freezing solid. With a dangerous list developing we managed to round up and steer a course by hand from the tiller-flat for Halifax where the ice was removed and steam heating fitted round the steering cables. We were still losing ships but the situation could have been worse were it not for those lovely people at Bletchley Park who laboured night and day deciphering the Enigma Code used by the German U-boat arm.

The came Convoy HX.229 from Halifax to UK and escorts were scarce. MANSFIELD was called out and in the company of H.M.S BEVERLEY, sailed to join the convoy on Friday 13 March 1943.

This date and day of sailing, caused much speculation to say the least. At this stage another Goole man George Walker, had joined MANSFIELD. As we sailed from the harbour, we passed the moorings of the River Class Frigate H.M.S TAY, which was commanded by Lieutenant-Commander Robert Sherwood R.N.R, a Goole man who was later described as the 'Nelson' of World War II by naval historical Captain W. Roskill D.S.C. RN.

Bletchley Park found that the U-boats had been ordered to fit an extra wheel in their Enigma Machines. This made the code virtually unreadable and gave them more luck than they were entitled to.

Several U-boat groups found the convoy HX.229 that consisted of 38 Merchant Ships and four escorts. There were 40 U-boats in the 'offing' and no assistance from shore. What followed was later called the most 'savage and ruthless sea battle of all time' by historians.

In the absence of the Group Leader the charge lead was taken by Lt. Cr. Luther in H.M.S VOLUNTEER.

The battle started on the night of the 15th. Several ships were hit including a tanker SOUTHERN PRINCESS that burned furiously. The light of the blaze attracted several U-boats to the scene.

It was decided against the normal practice, to pick up survivors from lifeboats, rafts, carley-floats. The sea was littered with the little red light of life-jackets. While this was going on and we were motionless in the water Capt. Erwin Christophersen in U-228 fired three torpedoes at MANSFIELD but all missed and with 150 survivors of different nationalities on board we rejoined the convoy. Eventually we were out of the air-gap and had some air cover. MANSFIELD was running short of fuel so left the convoy to proceed at economical speed to Gourock.

This was an uneventful passage except that a huge wave swept away a watch-keeper who lost his life. The fresh water evaporator, through trying to cope twice the output, was giving trouble. However we did arrive at Gourock and the cheers of the survivors as their train left the quay to us in no uncertain manner that we had done the right thing.

Wilhelmshaven

After loading roadstone at Rekkefjiord in Norway, Cairnleader arrived at Wilhelmshaven after an uneventful passage. Wilhelmshaven is the Historic Naval Base of the Navy of Germany and is very sacred ground. The lock opens on the landward side to the Naval Basin and it was here that Kapitan Leutnant Gunther Prien, Commander of U-Boat U-47,was recieved with great ceremony after the sinking of HMS Royal Oak at Scapa Flow in World War II.

In order to reach the discharging berth the Cairnleader had to navigate this sacred basin and on leaving the lock, visiting vessels were expected to steam reverentially through the dockyard at Dead Slow Ahead and dip the ensign in respect. On this occasion the dock pilot stood in the starboard wing of the bridge and I myself was stationed at the main engine control in the wheelhouse. Ian McEwan, the captain, stood in the wing of the bridge talking to the pilot. The pilot was giving engine movement orders to the captain who, instead of calling them to me, answered the pilot in conversational tones. To make matters worse the wireless in the chartroom, (integral with the wheelhouse), had been left on and tuned in to Radio 4, (used to be the Light Programme), which we used for the Shipping Weather Forecasts. As I could anticipate the first order I was able to lip-read and proceeded to Dead Slow Ahead. At this stage I called to the captain to switch off the wireless but to no avail and as we steamed reverentially through one of the most sacred streches of water in the world Radio 4 started blasting out the Dambusters March. The captain still conversing with the pilot and, as we proceeded thus, I felt a mixture of embarrassment, respect and a little amusement.

Kapitan Leutnant Gunther Prien of the U-47 being congratulated by U-boat Commodore Doenitz(centre), and Grand-Admiral Raeder(right), after returning to Wilhelmshaven from the sinking of the Royal Oak.

(7ad). **Alastair BRYDON** – Shipwright.

Alastair was born on 19th.July1932 at Edinburgh. After leaving school he served an apprenticeship as a carpenter with the Leith shipbuilders, Henry Robb Limited, at Leith Docks. He was conscripted into the Army as a carpenter serving with the R.E.M.E. stationed mostly on the Isle of Wight. He was demobbed with the rank of Corporal.

Alastair carried on with the tools of his trade. On 30th October,1959 he joined the Merchant Navy, serving with the Cairn Line of Steamships as a shipwright on CAIRNAVON(IV) until 25th February, 1960.   (3 voyages under Captain John Hogg).

Between 20th April,1960 and 10th August,1962. he served with Ellerman & Wilson Line of Hull, as shipwright on board the M.V. RAPALLO. (built by Henry Robb Ltd. at Leith Docks 3,402/60) for12 voyages. On 21st November,1961 whilst RAPALLO was lying at buoys at Istanbul, Turkey, it was struck and damaged by Italian motor vessel, SAN MARCO. (4,755/56. of the Adriatic Soc. Asper. Azioni- Di-Navigazione, Venice.) and the Turkish steamer MEHMENT IPAR (7,086/45 of Iparttransport Co. Ltd, Istanbul) both vessels drifting out of control due to high winds. He then sailed one voyage on the Clan Line steamer CLAN BUCHANAN,(9,909/41) until 14th November, 1962, when Alastair went ashore.

Alistair at hatch, to prepare boarding for cargo.

CHAPTER 8.

THE LAST OF THE LINE. . – The 'Mini-bulkers'

In 1892 with the order of the sister ships CAIRNAVON (1). & CAIRNMORE. the Cairn Line of Steamships Ltd began a successful policy of ordering their new tonnage in pairs, as sister ships, invariably from the same shipbuilders. This policy continued for the next seventy years, during which time the company took delivery, in total of 7 pairs of similar steamships, the last being in 1952 with the delivery of the two turbine driven steamers, CAIRNGOWAN (1V). & CAIRNDHU (1V). from the West Hartlepool yard of William Gray & Company Ltd.

It is not generally known, however that four years later, during 1956 and 1957, the Cairn Line, in a continuation of their 'twin vessel' ordering policy, again placed orders for two 7,500 tons, single screw, motor-ships. The Burntisland Shipbuilding Company Ltd, of Fife, were contracted to build both vessel, each to be fitted with a Doxford opposed piston diesel engine, a significant break with tradition, by the company.

The first vessel, CAIRNFORTH. ordered in April, 1956 and allocated Yard No.383. was completed in November, 1958. Remarkably, not only was she was the first and only diesel engined vessel ever built for the Cairn Line, but was also, the last ship, built for the company in its 129 years history, prior to the Furness Withy take over, in 1967. The contract for her proposed sister ship, signed 13 months later in May, 1957, was allocated Yard No. 397, for delivery in December,1961. In April, 1958, however, prior to any announcement of any proposed Cairn name, the order for this vessel was cancelled, not withstanding that preliminary construction work had already commenced at the Burntisland shipyard. The sudden cancellation also left engine builders, Hawthorn Leslie, with a partially erected 4 cylinder, 4SCSA. Doxford oil engine, on their hands, at their St. Peters Works on Tyneside. Not only did this situation mark the beginning of the end, for the Cairn Line of Steamships, but also contributed to the demise of the Burntisland Shipbuilding Company, Ltd. which went into liquidation in1969 following further order cancellations, after 51 years of shipbuilding on the Forth. .

The decision by Furness Withy in 1969, shortly after their takeover of the Cairn Line, to order a series of 10 'Mini bulk carriers of 1600 g.r.t. for use in the short sea bulk trades, and register them under the Cairn Line of Steamships banner, marked a distinct change of direction for both companies. No doubt brought about by the onset of containerisation, this shift in policy seems to have proved a success and under Shaw Savill & Albion's management, the fleet flourished, until 1983, by which time all ten ships had been sold on to various other companies, for further trading. Now over 30 years old, 8 out of 10 of these handy-size bulkers continue to trade, but by now must be reaching the end of their service life. Representing the only former Cairn Line owned vessels, now still at sea, an updated history of each of the 'Mini-bulkers' as of January, 2008, are appended below:

SHIPMAIR III. (Ex. CAIRNVENTURE). [Foto Flite.]

SSA. 1. **CAIRNVENTURE**. (1969 - 1974).

O.N.338899. IMO. 7000334. 1,436g. 883n. 2,600dwt. 254.5 x 39.1 x 14.4 feet.

8 cylinder 4 SCSA. (320mm x 450mm) oil engine by Atlas-MAK. Maschinenebau., GmbH..Kiel, Germany. 1,500 bhp.11.5 knots.

Steel hull, 2 decks. F.36. P.50 feet. 2x hatches,1 hold, 3,126.1 cu/b. 4 masts with only 4 derricks fitted.

12/1969. Completed by E.J. Smit & Zoon, Westerbroek, Netherlands. (Yard No. 792) for The Cairn Line of Steamships Ltd. Newcastle-upon-Tyne. (Shaw, Savill & Albion & Co. Mgrs.) London. U.K. flag. Chartered to Ellerman Lines Ltd, London.

1974. SHIPMAIR III. - Shipmair. BV. (Oost Atlantic Lijn). Rotterdam.

1976. PASSAAT SANTOS. – Scheepsvaart Maatschappij Passaat Santos. (Oost Atlantic Lijn.) Willemstad. N/A.

1977. ERIC. Handel Wijdzicht B.V. Rotterdam.

1979. GHADAMES. Lifestar Cia. Nav. SA. Greece. (Fereniki Lines, Mgrs.) Piraeus.

1986. ALEXIA. Brother Hood Shipping Co. Ltd (A. Economides Mgrs.).Cyprus.

1990. STAR QUEEN. Rainbow Shipping Co.SA. (A..Economides, Mgrs.) Cyprus.

1992. VEDIA. Occidental Cia. Nav.S.A. San Lorenzo. Honduras.

1992. SHEREEN A. Occidental Compania Nav.S.A.(Henry M. Diad, Mgrs.) Beirut.

7/11/1994. Abandoned on fire 5 miles West of Kea Island, Greece, on voyage from Ismir, Turkey for Italy. Towed into the Greek port of Laurium in burnt out condition. Declared a CTL

31/12/1995. Arrived Aliaga, Turkey for demolition.

1996. Sold on for further trading.

1996. MEHMET ASLAN. Honduras flag.

7/11/1997. Tilted up over pier at Bourgas Bulgaria, while loading 2,000 tons of bagged bentonite clay. Crew abandoned ship, holds half full with water. No casualties.

8/9/1998. Vessel still in abandoned position.

27/2/2002. Sold to Liberty Metals group, Bourgas..Bulgaria. and broken up.

KARIM 1. (Ex. CAIRNTRADER).   [Foto Flite.]

SSA.2. **CAIRNTRADER**. (1971 - 1976).
O.N.341239. IMO.7038537. 1,581g. 977n. 2,706dwt.   287. X 39.8 x 19.3 feet.
8 Cylinder 4 SCSA.(320mm x 450mm.) oil engine by Atlas-MAK. Maschinenebau GmbH. Keil.
Germany. 1,600 bhp.11.5 knots.
Steel hull. 2 decks. F.36. P.50 feet. 2 x hatches 1 hold. 3,126.1 cub. b. 4 masts with only 4 derricks
fitted.
1971. Launched as CAIRNTRADER by E.J. Smit Zoon, Westerbroek, Netherlands (Yard No. 795)
for The Cairn Line of Steamships Ltd. London. (Shaw, Savill Albion &. Co. Ltd, Mgrs.) London.
3/1971. Completed as SAXON PRINCE. On charter to the Prince Line.
1975. CAIRNTRADER. at end of Prince Line charter.
1976. SAXON PRINCE. Chartered to The Prince line,
1976. ADARA. Van Nievelt, Goudriaan & Co. B.V. Rotterdam. Dutch flag,
1986. ANDARA. Waterdrive Marine Ltd. Limassol, Cyprus.
1990. PARANA STAR. Interfront Shipping Ltd. Cyprus.(Rederi A/B. Hastings Mgrs.) St. Malmo,
Sweden.
1992. PAMELA. Astarte Shipping Ltd. Cyprus. (Humber Shipping, Mgrs.).
1995. ARANA. Shipdepot Ltd. St. Vincent & Grenadines. (Rederi.A/B. Hastings ,Mgrs) St. Malmo.
Sweden.
1996. KARIM 1. (One). Elreedy Shipping Co. Belize.
2003. KARIM I (Aye)   Elreedy Shipping Co. Egypt, under Cambodian flag.
19/5/2006. The Turkish flagged chemical tanker ZOPPUN.(3,451/80) was departing Constanta,
Turkey, lost main engine power and collided with the cargo ship KARIM 1 moored in the port area,
loaded with timber. KARIM 1. sustained a hole in her bow and was berthed alongside the Sorena
floating dock at Constanta for damage assessment.
29/5/2006. While docking for repairs to the collision damage, a week later, KARIM 1. sank after
water entered the hull through the hole in her bow. The crew of 12 Egyptians were all recued.
19/7/2006. Restored to an even keel after removal of deck fittings and refloated.
2/2007. Abandoned to the salvers Atriamar SRL. and sold for scrap.

MOUNTPARK. (Ex. CAIRNRANGER).   [Foto Flite.]

SSA.3. **CAIRNRANGER**. (1971 - 1976).

O.N.342952. IMO.7118076. 1,598g 1,008n 2,768dwt. 287. X 39.8 x 17.7 feet.

8 Cylinder 4SCSA. (320mm x 450mm) oil engine. Type.8M451AK.by Atlas -MAK Maschinenebau. GmbH. Kiel, Germany. 1,600 bhp. 11.5 knots.

Steel hull. 2 decks. 1 hold. F.53.1 P. 63 feet. Raised after deck. 51.2 feet.3,474.5 Cu.g.

Ice strengthened.

11/1971. Completed by E.J. Smit & Zoon, Westerbroek Netherlands, (Yard No.798) for The Cairn Line of Steamships Ltd.(Shaw Savill, Albion & Co.Ltd. Mgrs) London.

For Cairn Line service/routes.

1976. MOUNTPARK. Denholm Line Steamers Ltd.(J.& J.Denholm,Mgrs.) Glasgow.

1982. BENEDETTO SCOTTO. Salverina Varriale, Naples.

1988. MARYLAND. Sadav S.P.a, Italy.

1991. SAMER. Commer International, Kingston. St.Vincent & Grenadines .

1998. PIRGOS. Argo Maritime Ltd. (Bulgaria). St.Vincent & Grenadines flag.

2003. EDARTE II. Erada Shipping Co, Vlora. Albania. Albanian flag.

12/9/2005. VEGA. Albania.

30/11//2007. Still in service as VEGA..

VEGA. (Ex. CAIRNROVER).   [Foto Flite.]

SSA.4. **CAIRNROVER**. (1972 – 1978).
O.N.343094. IMO.7127974. 1,599g 1,009n. 2,768dwt. 287 x 39.8 x 17.7 feet.
8 Cylinder 4SCSA. (320mm x 450mm) oil engine Type 8M451AK. by Atlas- MAK. Maschinenebau.
GmbH. Kiel Germany. 1,600 bhp.11.5 knots.
Steel hull.2 decks. 1 hold F.53.1 P.63 feet. with raised quarter deck.51.2 feet. 3,474.5Cu.g.
Ice strengthened.
1972. Launched by N.V. Bodewes Scheepswerft, Martenshoek, Netherlands.(Yard No. 512) for
The Cairn Line of Steamships.(Shaw, Savill Albion & Co.Ltd. Mgrs.) London. for Cairn Line
service/routes.
1978. GIANNIS. White Palace Co. SA. (Konidaris Bros. Mgrs.). Greece. Greek flag.
1983. ANASTASSIA. Spartohorian Shipping Co. (Konidaris Bros. Mgrs.).Greece.
1986. ANASTASSIA ENA. New Haven Shipping Co. Ltd. Cyprus.
1986. REIDA. Angelamar di Coppola, Tommaso, Italy.
1993. STAR. Angelamar SAS.Monte di Procida, Italy.
2000. VEGA. Cargo Maritime Inc. St. Vincent & Grenadines.
2000. B. VENTURE. Trans Ocean Shipping, Panama City. Panamanian flag.
2001. ALDEBARAN V. Anquet Marine, Panama City, Panamanian flag.
2002. WAGIH 1. Bolivia. Bolivian flag.
2003. ALDEBAREN V. Anquet Marine, Panama City, Panamanian flag.
5/2007. Still in service as ALDEBAREN V.

LINDEWAL. (Ex. CAIRNLEADER). [Foto Flite.]

SSA.5. **CAIRNLEADER.** (1975 - 1982).

O.N.365924. IMO.7405077. 1,592g. 1,050n. 3,150dwt. 261. x 44.2 x 18.6 feet.

8 Cylinder 4 SCSA. (320mm x 450mm) oil engine. Type 8M452AK.by Atlas -MAK. Maschinenebau. GmbH. Kiel, Germany. 2,400 bhp. 12 knots.

Steel hull. 1 deck. 2 hatches. F.25.2 P.49.2 feet. 3,767 cu.G.

24/6/1975. Launched by Martin Jansen GmbH.& Co. K.G. Schiffswerke, Leer, Germany.(Yard No.132) for The Cairn Line of Steamships Ltd. (Shaw Savill, Albion & Co. Ltd, Mgrs.) London.

9/1975. Completed and chartered to The Prince Line. Same name and management.

Used on Cairn Line services/routes.

29/3/1977. On voyage from Pasajes for Glomfjord during early hours of the morning in heavy seas, rescued crew of six from a sinking yacht VERIC off Bordeaux and landed them at Gironde, for which Captain Milburn and crew were awarded medals and certificates for the rescue, by the French Authorities.

6/10/1982. LINDEWAL. H. P. Holwerda, Heerenveen, Netherlands.

1987. BENED. West Indian Shipping Co. Ltd. Limassol, Cyprus. (Holwerde Ship Management BV. Nederlands Mgrs,).

1988. MIRFAK. Marinymph Shipping Co. Ltd. Cyprus. ((Van Nievelt Goudriaan & Co. BV. Mgrs.) Rotterdam.

1989. FIVI. Hecate Shipping Co. Malta.

1990/91. Laid up.

1992. Sold to The Great Lakes Marine Co. Ltd. Panama. Same name.

2003. SENTINEL. Sea Sun Shipping SA. Comoros. (Sea Lord Maritime Mgrs.) Athens. Greece.

19/1/2004. Off register.

5/2007. Still in service as SENTINEL.

TJONGERWAL. (Ex. CAIRNFREIGHTER).   [Foto Flite.]

SSA. 6. **CAIRNFREIGHTER**. (1975 – 1982).
O.N. 365994.   IMO.7405089. 1,592 g 1.,050 n 3,150dwt.   261 x 44.2 x 18.6 feet.
8 Cylinder 4 SCSA.(320mm x 450mm) oil engine. Type 8M452AK by Atlas- MAK. Maschinenebau.
GmbH. Kiel, Germany.2,400 bhp. 12 knots.
Steel hull. 1 deck. 2 hatches. F.25.2 P.49.2. feet. 3,767cu.G.
29/9/1975. Launched by Martin Jansen GmbH. & Co. K.G. Schiffswerke, Leer. Germany.(Yard No.
133) for The Cairn Line of Steamships Ltd. (Shaw Savill, Albion & Co, Ltd, Mgrs) London. Used on
Cairn Line service/routes.
30/9/1978. Extensively damaged while at anchor in Flushing Roads. During bad weather was struck
by the cargo vessel AL-RAHIM (8,844/77) which had failed in an attempt to cross ahead of the
anchored ship and had collided with the port side causing damage to the bow, forecastle and foredeck.
Both vessels remained afloat and later repaired.
1982. TJONGERWAL. H.P. Holwerda, Heerenveen, Netherlands.
31/12/1984. At Sharpness Docks, while leaving berth after loading, collided with another Holwerda
vessel, GERA HOLWERDA.(1,598 /78) which was berthed ahead, also loading, at the at same quay.
Damage sustained by both ships. No casualties. Both subsequently repaired.
1987. CENED. Rhino Navigation & Co. Ltd. Limassol. Cyprus. (Holwerda Ship Management BV,
Nederlands Mgrs.).
1988. MEGREZ. Maymorn Shipping Co. Ltd. Cyprus.(Van Nievelt Goudriaan & Co. BV. Mgrs.).
1989. VILARO. Albamar S.S. di Luigi & Co. Naples. Italy.
1994. BLUE LINE. Med Transport S.R.I. Naples. Italy.
1996. DOMINICA. Intership Management & Bunker Trading Corp. Madeira, Portugal.
1999. ECUBEA. Feldon Business Ltd. Madeira, Portugal.
2001. TIKA. Four Seas Maritime Co. Ltd. (Four Seas Maritime, Mgr.) Phnom Phen. Cambodia.
18/11/2002. ABDULRAZZAK-A. Four Seas Maritime Co. Ltd. (Douaa Shipping. Mgrs) Tartous,
Syria. Cambodian flag. POR. Phnom Phen.
9/6/2003. ABDULRAZZAK A. Four Seas Maritime Co. Ltd. (Douaa Shipping. Mgrs).Tartous,
Syria. Cambodian flag. POR. Phnom Phen.
1/2007. Still in service as ABDULRAZZAK A.   Under Russian register.

TEQUILA SUNSET. (Ex. CAIRNCARRIER).   [Foto Flite.]

SSA.7. **CAIRNCARRIER.** (1976 - 1982).

O.N. 366041.   IMO.7405091. 1,592 g. 1,050n. 3,150dwt.   261 x 44.2 x 18.6 feet.

8 Cylinder 4 SCSA.(320mm x 450mm) oil engine. Type 8M452AK. by Atlas- MAK. Maschinenebau GmbH. Kiel, Germany. 2,400 bhp. 12 knots.

Steel hull. 1 Deck. 2 hatches. F. 25.2 P.49.2 feet. 3,767 cu.G.

2/10/1975. Keel Laid.

5/12/1975. Launched by Martin Jansen GmbH. & Co. K.G. Schiffswerke. Leer, Germany.(Yard No. 134) for The Cairn Line of Steamships Ltd. (Shaw Savill, Albion & Co. Ltd. Mgrs.) London. Used on Cairn Line services/routes.

3/2/1976. Completed.

1982. TEQUILA SUNSET. Tequila Maritime SA. Panama.

1984. ARKLOW BRIDGE. Joint ownership of Shiel & Byrne Ltd and Arklow Shipping Ltd. Arklow. Ireland. (Arklow Shipping Ltd. Mgrs.).

1988. Sold to Shiel & Byrne Overseas Ltd. Dublin. (Arklow Shipping Mgrs.) Arklow Name unchanged.

1990. WAVE ROSE. Boterita Shipping SA.(Navimar SA. Mgrs) Panama.

1990. Navimar S.A.removed as managers.

1993. ARMOUR. Samer Maritime. (Successors Shipping SA. Mgrs) Panama.

1997. EUROLINK. Night Flare Navigation SA. (Sigma Maritime Inc. Mgrs.) Panama.

2001. Managers re-styled: International Maritime, Greece.

23/8/2004. VARUN. Mongolian owners.

12/10/2004. MIRAGE. Belize flag.

16/5/2005. NAJIB M. Middle East Work & Supplies (Memswo Mgrs.) Beirut. Lebanon. Comoros flag.

2006. NAJIB. Comoros flag.

5/2007.Still trading as NAJIB.

Note: The fourth vessel in this class of seven vessels built by Martin Jansen GmbH. & Co. Schiffswerke at Leer was ordered by The Cairn Line of Steamships but sold on the stocks to P. A.van Es.& Co. Rotterdam. and entered their service as BREEZAND.

ST. ANTON. (Ex. CAIRNASH).   [Foto Flite.]

SSA.8. **CAIRNASH**. (1976 - 1983).
O.N.377143.   IMO.7405649.   1,597 g 1,169 n. 3,171 dwt. 275.1 x 46 x 18.4 feet.
Post 1983:Increased dimensions: 2,300 g 1,413 n 4,028 dwt. 301. x 46 x 19.8 feet.
12 Cylinder 4 SCSA (300mm x 450 mm) Fiat oil engine.Type GMT. by H. Cegielski, Poznan, Poland.
geared to a single controllable pitch propeller. 2,500 bhp. 13.5 knots.
Steel hull. 1 Deck. 2 hatches. F.30.2. P.54.1 feet. 3,490.cu.G. as completed.
30/9/1976. Launched by Stocznia Gdanska, Lenina, Poland.(Yard No. B.473/01) for The Cairn Line of
Steamships Ltd,(Shaw Savill Albion & Co. Ltd. Mgrs) London.
12/1976. Completed.
1/1977. Delivered.
1983. ANDREA. Peter Cremer, Singapore.   Vessel lengthened.
1985. ST. ANTON. Minibulk Schiffswert GmbH.& Co. K.G. (Osterreichischer Lloyd /Krohn
Shipping Group Mgrs) Vienna, Austria.
2000. LEOPARD. Bulk Traders International, Phnom Phen, Cambodia.
2004. NOUR- A. Steadfast Shipping, Marshall Islands. (Hiba Shipping, Mgrs.) Syria. Comoros flag.
10/1/2007. Still in service as NOUR-A.

GUEPARD. (Ex. CAIRNELM).   [Foto Flite.]

.

SSA.9. **CAIRNELM**. (1977 - 1983)
O.N.377161.   IMO.7405651, 1,597 g 1,169 n 3,171dwt.   275.1 x 46. X 18.4 feet.
Post 1983:Incresed dimensions: 2,300 g 1,413 n 4,028 dwt. 301. X 46. X 19.8 feet.
12 Cylinder 4 SCSA (300mm x 450mm) Fiat Oil engine.Type GMT. by H. Cegielski, Poznan, Poland
geared to a single controllable pitch propeller. 2,500 bhp. 13.5 knots. Steel hull. 1 Deck. 2 hatches.
F.30.2 P.54.1 feet. 3,490 cu. G as delivered.
19/10/1976. Launched by Stocznia Gdanska, Lenina. Poland. (Yard No.B473/02) for The Cairn Line
of Steamships Ltd. (Shaw Savill Albion & Co. Ltd. Mgrs) London.
1/1977. Completed.
1983. CHRISTIANE. Peter Cremer, Singapore. Vessel lengthened.
1985. ST. CHRISTOPH Minibulk Schiffswert GmbH. & Co.K.G. (Osterreichischer Lloyd/Krohn
Shipping Group Mgrs.) Vienna, Austria.
20/6/2001. Damaged in collision West bound in English Channel when the bow of the on coming
M.V.KONGA. collided with the stern of the ST. CHRISTOPH. with both ships were travelling in the
same direction, in the lane separation system. Slight damage to both vessels.
2001. GUEPARD. Bulk Traders International , Phnom Phen. Cambodia.
2002. Owners restyled 'Guepard' Marine.Phnom Phen. Cambodian flag. Same name.
2003. Sold to Bulk Traders International, Barbados flag. Same name.
2004. Sold to' Guepard' Marine(Consolidated Bulk) Lebanon. Barbados flag. Same name.
2/2007. BAYOUT. Alexandre Maritime, Lebanon. (Chekka Shipping Mgrs.) Athens. Lebanese flag.
11/2007. Still in service as BAYOUT.

ST. JACOB. (Ex. CAIRNOAK). [Foto Flite.]

SSA.10. **CAIRNOAK**. (1977 - 1983).
O.N.377181. IMO 7405663. 1,597 g. 1,169 n. 3,171 dwt. 275.9 x 46 x 18.4 feet.
Post1983: Increased dimensions:2,300 g 1,413 n, 4,028 dwt. 301. x 46 x 19.8 feet.
12 Cylinder 4 SCSA (300mm x 450mm) Fiat oil engine Type GMT. by H. Cegielski, Poznan, Poland.,
geared to a single controllable pitch propeller. 2.600 bhp. 13.5 knots.
Steel hull. 1 Deck. 2 hatches. F.30.2 P. 54.1 feet. 3,490 cu.G. as delivered.
16/11/1976. Launched by Stocznia Gdanska, Lenina, Poland.(Yard No. B/473/03) for The Cairn Line
of Steamships Ltd. (Shaw Savill, Albion & Co. Ltd. Mgrs). London.
2/1977. Completed & delivered.
1983. LEONY. Peter Cramer. Singapore. Vessel lengthened.
1985. ST.JAKOB. Minibulk Schiffswert GmbH. & Co. K.G. (Osterreichischer Lloyd/Krone
Shipping Group Mgrs.) Vienna, Austria.
2000. JAKOB. Ronel Shipping Inc. Cork. Ireland. St. Vincent & Grenadines.
9/2/2004. Sold to Jakob Shipping, St. Vincent & Grenadines., (H.H. Brothers Maritime, Mgrs) Varna,
Bulgaria. St. Vincent & Grenadine flag. Same Name.
5/2007. Still in service as JAKOB.

Chapter 11.

THE CAIRN LINE OF STEAMSHIPS . 1876 – 2005.
ISBN 0 – 9550078 – 0 -1.   First published in 2005.

———————————————————

ADDITIONS AND AMENDMENTS. (List for inclusion in ' MEMORIES OF THE CAIRN LINE OF STEAMSHIPS and NAUTICAL TALES BEYOND LEITH.

———————————————————-

Page.27. Amend : VESPASION to read VESPACIAN.

Page.30. Amend: CAIRNROSS(III) to CAIRNROSS (II). caption under plan.

Page.37. Amend: MOSSDALE to read MOSDALE.

Page.45. Additional Info: Re: CAIRNGOWAN(1) - after KATTEGAT. insert
        (1,848g/1935).

Page.48.Additional Info: Re: CAIRNISLA. Insert:
10/1912. - 1914. Chartered to John Holt & Company Ltd. Liverpool and used on their Liverpool/West Africa service carrying general cargo out-mahogany logs on return.

Page.52. Re: CAIRNAVON (II) The photograph shown is of CAIRNAVON(IV) and not CAIRNAVON(II) as it should be.

Page.52. Additional Info: re CAIRNNEVIS - Insert:
22/1/1938. Captured in Straits of Gibraltar by the Spanish Nationalist auxiliary cruiser MALLORCA. (2,223/1914) ,while running cargo to Spanish Republican forces, during the Spanish Civil War. Subsequently condemned as a 'war prize' and interred into the Spanish Government fleet and renamed SEVILLA.

Page.53. Additional Info: CAIRNRONA. Inset: After
'Completed 5/8/1900' insert ' Sailed Hull same day on maiden voyage to New York.'
1/3/1908. Sailed from Hull for Boston and New York on her last voyage for the Wilson Line of Hull, before purchase by Cairn-Thomson Line.

1/1/1910.-25/1/1910 .First 'Cairn Thomson' voyage from London to St.Johns N/Scotia. 1/3/1910. – 11/3/1910. Second voyage from London to St. Johns. N.S.
30/4/1910. Suffered fire etc.

Page.54. Additional Info: DEVONA. Insert:
6/1907. Collided with iceberg in fog 130 miles East of Belle Isle on voyage from Montreal for London, sustaining damage to the forepeak and No.1 hold which filled with water and discarded part of its cargo. Hull sustained a lengthy fracture to the port side, which resulted in the vessel to returning to Montreal for repairs.

Page.54. Additional Info: FREMONA. Insert:
13/5/1896. Collided with an iceberg 20 miles South of Cape St. Mary's on a voyage from Montreal for Dundee, sustaining damage to port bow, which was holed. Put into
North Sydney. N.S. for repairs.

Page.56. Additional Info: CAIRNGOWAN(II). Insert:
4/4/1914. Struck iceberg 300 miles S.E. of Cape Race. on a voyage from Middlesbrough for Montreal. Partial damage. Arrived Montreal under own power for repairs.

Page.58. Additional Info: CAIRNMONA. (II).Insert:
30/10/1939. Torpedoed and sunk by U.13. 3 miles N.E. of Rattray Head, the last ship in South bound convoy, HX.5. on voyage from Montreal/ Halifax for Leith /Tyne with a cargo of wheat and copper. Forty two survivors picked up by the Royal Navy drifter. HMS RIVER LOSSIE. (202g/1920). 3 engine room crew lost.

Page.58. Amend: CAIRNVALONA.
Amend tonnages to read '4,666g. 2,806n.'

Page.59. Additional Info: CAIRNDHU.(III). Insert:
27/2/1925. Extensively damaged in a collision in Blyth harbour, while loading coal under the drops, by a collier manoevering at an adjoining berth, causing extensive damage to hull plating. Damage repairs carried out by Cowpen Dry Dock Company, Blyth, and returned to service.
1931/35. Laid up at River Tyne. Sold to the Greek' Livanos group' out of lay-up.
Page.60. Additional info: CAIRNROSS.(III).
Amend. 6/1/1940. to 17/1/1940. Insert. 'All 48 crew saved and picked up by Royal Navy destroyer H.M.S. MACKAY (D.70) and landed at Liverpool.'

Page.61. Additional Info: CAIRNESK.(III). Insert:
6/1948. Refit and alterations. River Tyne. Additional cabins for 11 passengers constructed on No.1 deck, either side of the existing deck house enclosing the main deck space below the bridge deck. Radar set fitted for the first time..

Page.62. Additional Info: CAIRNGLEN.(II). Insert:
17/7/1937. Collided with iceberg in Straits of Belle Isle, inbound from Newcastle /Leith for Montreal. Minor damage only. No casualties.
20/7/1937. Arrived safely at Montreal.

Page.71. Additional info: SCHIAFFINO FRERES /CAIRNAVON.(V).
Amend to Yard No. 632, Insert:
8/4/1972. Arrived Istanbul, Turkey for demolition.

Page.74. Additional Info: LINDFIELD.
Delete '2003. Still in service ' and Insert:
3/6/1998. Laid up at Falmouth.
24/4/1999. Arrived Mumbai for demolition.

Chapter 12.

<u>EPILOGUE</u>.

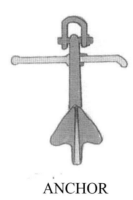

ANCHOR

Thinking back on my career a friend once told me, I had only spent 5 minutes in the Merchant Navy. Fair comment-considering a seafarers career, could last up to 50 years before 'swallowing the anchor.

However in my '5 minutes' I experienced many events, which I may have not seen otherwise. Most were natural, some were unexplainable, and a few happened-which shouldn't have!

I enjoyed sea life, but unfortunately had to leave for personnel and family reasons.

During my working life with regard to my 'four careers' I penned the following paraphrase:

Life's smallest decisions can make, break or change our evaluation of life. It seldom follows its intended course or our perceived anticipation of its outcome. So when a crossroad is reached trust in your decision to follow the correct path at the correct time in the correct manner in order to achieve total fulfilment in your life.

G.T.W.

NOTES

Author: Gilbert T. Wallace.

Author of the previously published 'Cairn Line of Steamship Co. Ltd. 1876 – 2005.' he attended Leith Nautical College, Edinburgh, prior to joining the 'Cairn Line of Steamships' in 1949, as a cadet. In 1954 he enlisted with the Royal Air Force, serving as a Military Policeman with the RAF (Provost) Police until1957 when he resigned to join The City of Edinburgh Police. Completion of his Police service in 1988 found him employed by The Crown Office, in Edinburgh for a further ten years. He finally retired in 1998 and still lives in Edinburgh with his wife.